To Nick – Ve———————s

Hope y—
cooking ———
– look no fish!
Janet + Tony

JUST LIKE MUM USED TO MAKE

CLASSIC RECIPES

JUST LIKE MUM USED TO MAKE

CLASSIC RECIPES

Laura Mason &
Sara Paston-Williams

National Trust

This edition published for WHSmith in 2014 by
National Trust Books
10 Southcombe Street
London W14 0RA

An imprint of Anova Books Ltd

ISBN 9781907892875

A CIP catalogue record for this book is available from the
British Library.

20 19 18 17 16 15 14
8 7 6 5 4 3 2 1

Reproduction by Mission Productions Ltd, Hong Kong
Printed by CT Printing, China

Photography by Tara Fisher
Home economy by Jane Suthering
Styling by Wei Tang

Picture credits: Page 10 and 170 © National Trust Images/ Paul Harris;
34 © NTI / Myles New; 56 and 170 © NTI/ James Dobson; 82 © NTI/
David Levenson; 89 © NTI / Ross Hoddinott; 106 © Gerard Lacz /
FLPA; 124 © NTI/ John Millar.

Contents

Introduction

A ROAST IS A CLASSIC BRITISH RECIPE. Much more than a hunk of meat cooked in a certain way. Think of a roast and we think of vast joints of beef turning on spits in front of huge fires, of venison poached from under the gamekeeper's nose, of medieval boards groaning under the weight of peacocks, swans and sucking pigs, of Christmas geese and turkeys, and of convivial Sunday dinners. In short, a roast is an idea of plenty, of feasting (legitimate or otherwise), and of occasion. Over the years, this has been allowed to decline into the bland reality of gravy granules and ready meals.

A roast is worth more than that. Meat is a resource that is likely to become scarcer – and well-produced meat even more so. We should value it properly for what it is – a food in which months, or possibly years, of an animal's life is concentrated into a package of protein and fat, at once nourishing and delicious, an excuse for a gathering, and provider of meals to come.

Good meat for a roast is expensive and, to some extent, a luxury. This is how it should be – as, too, should be the ability to use meat left over from one meal to make another, equally appealing meal. An element of a long-held idea that British meat is so good that it needs no 'messing about' still persists, but before the 19th century strong flavours were appreciated, as they are once again. Many of the ideas given here try to capture flavours of the past, using as inspiration recipes from historic cookery texts that would undoubtedly have found their way into the kitchens of houses now owned by the National Trust. Also included are a few forays into current fashions.

Family Roasts

A roast forms a special part of British eating habits, even if it is not quite the weekly punctuation mark it once was. Changes in taste and lifestyle have influenced how people eat; but a well-chosen piece of meat, carefully cooked, is an opportunity for conviviality, a gathering of family and friends.

Seasonings and accompaniments for roasts have changed over the centuries, from medieval combinations of spices, through tastes for citrus and anchovies, and rich meaty concoctions, to the 'plain cookery' of the late 19th century; our adoption of Mediterranean and Asian flavours is another link in this chain. Some items that have shown remarkable persistence are bread sauce, mustard, apple sauce, sage and onion, and redcurrant jelly, all established in the way that we use them today by the 18th century. We look for potatoes to accompany our roasts, but until the end of that century our ancestors would have expected pudding, perhaps a spherical, breadcrumb-and-flour plum one, or a batter type, still with us as Yorkshire pudding.

Sourcing a Roast

The first rule of good roasting is to buy good meat. The British Isles and Ireland have long been recognised for producing excellent meat, especially beef and mutton, but many factors other than simply 'buying British' come under consideration – flavour, price, animal welfare, place of origin. A roast from a supermarket can produce a reasonable meal, but one from a butcher or sourced directly from a farmer is likely to give something much better. Some suppliers are expensive, but others may be cheaper than supermarkets, and a knowledgeable supplier is likely to be able to tell you more about the animals.

Meat lies at the end of the food chain and represents a concentrated and precious food resource. The idea that it should be cheap is erroneous, and on balance it is better to pay a bit more for something well produced and to eat a bit less.

Where to Buy Meat

Who is likely to sell good meat for roasting? To some extent, finding a good supplier needs trial and error. When buying from a supermarket, look for premium lines that are sourced from specified areas, breeds, groups of farms, or which are given some kind of special treatment (such as proper hanging). Read the labels. The price will almost certainly be a premium one as well. The more anonymous the meat is, the less likely it is to have been raised with care. Some of the best meat producers work on a very small scale. To find meat for a good roast, the internet, local producer groups, and food and drink festivals are all good sources of information.

Alternatively, try to find a butcher you trust, and then cultivate him or her. Good butchers will be able to provide much more than a slice of rump steak and a couple of chops. They should be able to prepare a joint neatly, deboning it if asked (then giving the bones to you along with the meat, of course); do any trimming and tying as necessary; and be able to provide extra beef or pork fat should the meat require it. Most butchers take great pride in the quality of the meat they sell, and specialise in meat from particular animal breeds or areas.

General Information on Cuts of Meat

When you have found a supplier, what should you buy? With a very few exceptions (such as a small rack of lamb), it is a waste of time to roast any piece of meat weighing less than 1kg (2¼ lb). If the roast is just for two, then there will be leftovers, and there are plenty of dishes to make with those. As a very basic rule of thumb, allow about 125g (4½ oz) per person for meat off the bone and 250g (9oz) per person for meat on the bone, but don't be too exact about this, especially if the meat is for an occasion when a really handsome piece will make the party extra-special,.

The most sought-after roasts are what are known as 'prime cuts', which have a large proportion of tender lean meat and little, or relatively little, connective tissue. They come mostly from the hindquarters of animals. There is a limited supply and a lot of demand, so they are expensive. Secondary cuts, such as shoulder of pork or shoulder of lamb or mutton, are quite fatty with complex muscle structure and more connective tissue; these still make good roasts, but they don't carve as elegantly. Beef brisket and breast of veal, lamb or mutton are well flavoured; they have a layered structure that can make them chewy, but still make good family meals. Belly pork, which might also be considered, is more tender and seems to be enjoying a revival of interest at present. In general terms, when buying fresh meat that is cut to order, look at the colour of the meat and the texture of the fat, and avoid meat with a lot of juice running from it, or that has an unpleasant smell.

Bones in meat help to conduct heat, so may shorten cooking times a little. They add flavour, especially to gravy, and are very useful for making stock and can look impressive when the meat comes to the table. On the other hand, they make carving more complex, especially in joints such as shoulder of lamb or mutton. Joints such as rack of lamb and loin of pork should be chined – that is, part of the backbone removed – making them easier to carve. Most joints can be boned and rolled by the butcher on request (if you don't feel equal to the task), leaving a cavity suitable for stuffing. Take the bones home for the stockpot.

Fatty meat has been considered a public enemy by nutritionists for many years, and eating too much fat is certainly not a good idea. But leanness can be overdone too. A roasting joint needs fat; it is fat that gives flavour to meat, and prevents it becoming dry during cooking. Some will be present in layers on the outside of the piece, or between individual muscles; 'marbling' will be visible as streaks and flecks of fat in the lean meat, especially in beef. If fat worries you, remember that some of it will cook out of the meat during roasting and can be skimmed off the juices and then discarded. Visible fat can be cut off your own portion, but don't expect everyone to follow your example.

Roasting Equipment

A sturdy tin, of the heaviest gauge metal you can afford, is essential, especially if you plan to roast meat on a regular basis. Tins come in a range of sizes, from small chop roasters to ones that will hold a medium-sized turkey. Use a tin just large enough to hold the joint comfortably, with a little space around it to allow for basting. If the tin is too large, the cooking juices will dry out and burn. A range of materials is also available: anodised aluminium is a good option if heavy steel is too expensive. A light, thin metal tin will do the job of containing the meat in the oven, but it will warp sooner or later Once a tin has warped, the cooking juices will pool at one end and dry up and burn at the other, and it won't be much use. For chickens, and for slow-roasting and pot-roasting boned and rolled meat, a deep cast-iron pot with a lid is useful.

Ovens, Temperatures and Time

Getting to know your oven is important for producing a perfect roast. The quirks of individual ovens make it difficult to predict exact cooking times and temperatures. The all-round 'soaking' heat of Agas and similar stoves makes them very good for slow, even, thorough cooking. Electric ovens are generally even in temperature throughout, and manufacturers make claims about the efficiency of fan-assisted ones. Gas ovens can be blazing hot at the top and cooler at the bottom, meaning that items must be moved around on the shelves during cooking. If you lack confidence with a new oven, begin with something good-natured and relatively simple – a piece of slow-roast pork, or a boned shoulder of lamb – and eat it with new potatoes. There is no point getting hot and bothered over a huge and expensive sirloin of beef, Yorkshire pudding and roast potatoes.

As a rule, beef, lamb, mutton and game may be cooked to any stage between rare and well done, depending on taste, but pork and poultry should always be fully cooked. Joints of meat vary in weight and shape, and people vary in the extent to which they like meat cooked. Prime cuts can be cooked quickly at high temperatures, but lesser ones need longer roasting at lower temperatures. Roasting time for meat is often calculated by allowing a certain amount of time per pound of meat, multiplied by the weight of the joint; this rule of thumb was worked out about 150 years ago when imperial measurements were the norm, and to convert it to metric, one has to remember that 500g is roughly equivalent to 1lb.

Meat Thermometers

One way to make sure a joint is cooked is to use a meat thermometer. Insert it into a thick part of the roast before it goes in the oven (make sure it's not touching any bones) and check the reading as cooking progresses. Probe thermometers are also available – these cannot be put in the oven, but can be used to take a reading of the internal temperature of the meat if it is removed from the oven. Again, avoid any bones when using these, and withdraw the probe slowly.

Classic Puddings

The British tradition for delicious puddings is centuries old. Puddings, pies, trifles and tarts have all been served regularly since medieval times and puddings are an integral part of Britain's culinary heritage. In recent years British food has enjoyed a well-deserved revival and, indeed, puddings are some of our great national dishes.

No book of Classic Recipes would be complete without a selection of both homely and heart-warming hot puddings and delicious cold tarts and flans. Our traditional puddings are glorious - rich, indulgent and comforting. Naughty? Yes, but oh so nice!

Beef & Veal

BEEF HAS LONG stood for all things good about food in England, excellent in quality and abundant in supply. To celebrate extraordinary events, whole oxen were roasted, as on the ice of the Thames during the Frost Fairs of the 17th and 18th centuries. On a domestic scale, a roast sirloin or rump of beef was considered the best of food. Privileged aristocrats and their French cooks had game and fancy dishes – but plain beef was the natural food of the upstanding Englishman.

The motif of roast beef appears again and again, in cartoons, prints, in the kitchen scenes depicted in recipe books, in menus real and imagined. Henri Misson in 1719 said of the English that 'two Dishes are their Dinners; a Pudding for instance, and a Piece of Roast Beef'. Later that century, the Norfolk parson James Woodforde was serving the same combination to his tenants for Christmas dinner. Roast beef and Yorkshire pudding is still an ideal Sunday dinner. The pudding might once have been a plum pudding, and now it's always Yorkshire – but the beef remains.

Before railways, the demand for beef was fed by cattle from Scotland, northern England and Wales, driven on foot to fatten in richer southern pastures, sold through the cattle fairs, such as Manningtree, and eventually reaching London. Further back than that, oxen were also important as draught animals, fattened for food only when pensioned off. Beef must have been deeper in flavour (and possibly tougher) than we are now accustomed to. It also appears to have been fatter, judging from some of the 18th-century depictions. During this century, agricultural improvers concentrated on selective breeding for meat or milk, producing beasts of great size. This was the genesis of 'traditional' British breeds that are still valued as meat animals – Beef Shorthorns, Herefords, Aberdeen Angus and others.

In the 19th century, beef – and meat generally – was given extra importance by the infant science of nutrition. Protein was emphasised, and for a while it was thought that all the 'goodness' of beef could be extracted in bouillon and beef tea. The idea was given a commercial push by manufacturers who reduced beef stock by boiling it to a pasty substance, which was packaged in tins – the origin of beef extract (still with us as Oxo and Bovril), and gravy mixes.

Traditional breeds remained the norm well into the 20th century. Many areas of the UK were recognised as producing excellent grass-fed beef – lowland Scotland, much of northern England and Northern Ireland, less hilly parts of Wales and the Welsh borders, parts of Sussex and Devon. These animals take a long time to reach the optimum weight for meat and are short in the back, so have relatively less of the prime meat used for roasts and steaks than continental breeds introduced in the 1960s. This was a disadvantage when tastes began to change in the late 1960s and nutritionists cautioned against large amounts of red meat and particularly its associated saturated fat. Beef also became more expensive and the BSE epidemic damaged the image of British beef.

Eliza Acton's observation in 1855 that ribs, sirloin and rump were the proper joints of beef for roasting still holds good. These all come from the back of the animal. Sirloin (from the French *sur*, meaning over or upon the loin) has always been prized. It was usually served as a plain roast, although a method known as hashing is described in 18th-century cookery books. When almost roasted, the layer of fat on top of the meat was raised, and the lean meat cut out except around the edges; the meat was finely minced with flavourings and replaced, the fat skewered back down. To us, this seems like an extravagant way of ruining a joint, but it was probably delicious. The long, tender 'undercut', located underneath the bones of a sirloin and better known to us as fillet steak, was usually left in place and carved with the rest of the joint, but sometimes it was removed, larded or stuffed and roasted or braised, a dish called 'mock hare'.

How the meat of the hindquarter – the rump – was divided in the past is less well known. There are plenty of instructions for roasting a rump or buttock of beef, but it is not clear exactly what was meant. It was obviously a very large piece, weighing up to 7kg (15lb). How closely this coincided with the current definition of rump of beef and adjacent cuts such as topside, thick flank and silverside isn't known, but the chump end (which equates to the meat now used for rump steaks) was certainly used as a roast. Two rumps together with the sirloins, still joined together, made a baron of beef – a cut now unavailable, since BSE legislation requires all cattle to be split down the backbone and the spinal cord removed. Roasts from the forequarter have probably always been similar to those used now – rib roasts and sometimes brisket.

Attitudes to veal are more ambivalent than those towards beef. The fact that Britain has plenty of pastureland available all year round for keeping cattle may have encouraged a preference for beef, but veal was eaten as well. Pastureland is not infinite, and some calves (especially in areas that concentrated on cheese-making) have always been culled. Veal used to be a sought-after ingredient, especially in French-influenced *haute cuisine*. But over the years, and especially in the 20th century, welfare concerns were raised about the conditions in which veal calves were raised, demand fell, and veal can be difficult to buy today.

During the 18th and 19th centuries, veal cuts were close to the ones still used. Flank of veal was sometimes turned into a 'veal goose' by spreading it with sage and onion stuffing, after which it was roasted and served with brown gravy and apple sauce, 'a convenient mode of dressing the flank …for eaters who do not object to the somewhat coarse savour of the preparation', remarked Eliza Acton rather sniffily when quoting a 'City of London receipt'. It was usual to stuff veal and serve it with sharp sauces to counteract a tendency to dryness and the bland nature of the meat. The old quality marker of whiteness in the meat was partly cosmetic (for recipes where the pale meat provided a contrast to some other ingredient) and partly a desire for delicacy in flavour – though this could be taken to the point of blandness.

Buying Beef and Veal Cuts for Roasting

Roasting beef is as much about cooking good meat by the correct method for the cut, as about recipes. Excellent beef is best bought from a good butcher; the best comes from dedicated beef herds grazing on open pasture and will have been allowed to hang for at least three weeks. The lean should be a good, deep red colour (not bright red) and lightly marbled – flecked with streaks of fat. The visible fat should be creamy-white and crumbly in texture.

Veal is a by-product of the dairy industry; anyone who drinks milk or eats cheese, butter, yoghurt or ice cream should not object to eating this meat. Although milk-fed veal at 2½–3 months old is still considered the best, there is an alternative: this is 'rosy', or rosé, veal, a deep pink colour with a light streaking of fat in between the muscles. It comes from older, loose-housed or outdoor-reared calves. Tracking it down takes persistence, and once you find it, you may have to order roasting joints. A butcher who deals with the catering trade, or the internet, are the most likely sources.

What to Buy, and How Much

The British method of butchering beef and veal tends to run across major muscle groups, cutting through fat and bone (rather than dissecting muscles out, which tends to be the practice in continental Europe). In the past, the names for cuts varied quite a lot regionally, although they appear to be fairly standard now.

Sirloin is expensive, and if you want a piece from the rear end of the joint with the fillet still in place, you may have to order it: the joint is more profitable when divided into sirloin, fillet and T-bone steaks. Working forwards, the front part of the sirloin is also known as the wing rib, with a good eye of lean meat but no undercut. Attached to this is the forerib, with streaks and layers of fat in the 'tail', getting progressively less lean. These joints respond well to fast roasting at relatively high temperatures. Buy sirloin by weight, and rib joints by number of ribs, although they can be boned and rolled (which makes them easier to carve, but less splendid at the table). Brisket (boned and rolled) has an excellent flavour, but is highly variable in size and fat content, and tends towards toughness. Be guided by the butcher's opinion, and treat it gently, with long, slow cooking. Working back from the sirloin, the next cut is the rump, now principally used for steaks; behind this, at the top of the hind leg, lies topside, a very lean piece of meat that makes a good slow roast; and next to it the silverside and a muscle known as the pope's eye, also possible roasting joints. These need to be slow roasted or pot roasted.

Veal cuts for roasting include loin (equivalent of the sirloin in beef cattle) and, the chump end or fillet and topside; towards the head, the best end (equivalent to a beef rib roast) and shoulder; the breast can also be boned and rolled with stuffing. Veal is lean and tends to dry out, so treat it gently and use a slow-roast method with secondary cuts.

Storage and Preparation

The British have traditionally considered that any home-produced roasting beef is full of flavour and far too good to be 'messed around with' – i.e., marinated or otherwise flavoured before cooking – and that when cooked appropriately, the meat will also be sufficiently tender. As far as flavourings are concerned, beef fillet (less pronounced in flavour than many cuts) can benefit from short marinating with oil and herbs, and light spicing makes an interesting change with slow-roast cuts. Otherwise, restrict seasonings to salt and pepper, and possibly a little mustard powder mixed with plain flour and rubbed into the fat of a sirloin or rib roast before cooking. Very lean beef, such as topside, benefits from barding with extra fat. Veal has a delicate flavour that is easily overpowered by strong seasonings. Good contrasts are light, lemony notes; salted meat such as ham or bacon; the nutty flavours of some fortified wines; and a mild mustard of the Dijon type. Stuffings are a good idea with veal. Because it is from young animals without much fat, veal can be dry. To help prevent this, bard with pork fat or spread a little butter over it before cooking. If you can obtain some veal bones (even in relatively small quantities) and use them to make stock, these will enhance veal gravy and many other dishes.

Times and Temperatures

How 'done' should roast beef be? Some people hate well-done beef; others don't like to see pink in the middle. In the mid-20th century, well-done meat seems to have been the norm, but since the 1980s, chefs and cookery writers have shown a very definite preference for underdone meat generally. If you are intending to use some of the beef cold or for leftovers, it's better if it is kept slightly rare. Very lean cuts of beef, such as topside, are better if they are done on the rare side of medium, because they tend to dry out during prolonged cooking. Really, it's a matter of taste.

There are two basic methods for roasting beef. The first is sometimes known as high-heat or fast roasting. For a fast roast, give the meat 20 minutes at 240°C, 475°F, Gas mark 9, then reduce the heat to 180°C, 350°F, Gas mark 4 and cook for the following times:
- Beef on the bone: 15 minutes per 500g (rare); 18–20 minutes per 500g (medium); 25 minutes per 500g (well done).
- Boneless beef: 12 minutes per 500g (rare); 13–15 minutes per 500g (medium); 20 minutes per 500g (well done).

The second method is slow roasting. Cook at 150°C, 300°F, Gas mark 2 for the entire time, allowing 20–25 minutes per 500g for rare to medium, and 30–35 minutes per 500g for well-done meat. Cook pot roasts even more slowly, at 140°C, 275°F, Gas mark 1, and up to 60 minutes per 500g.

Veal, because it tends to dryness, needs gentle heat. It should always be well done, but be careful not to overcook. Start it at 190°C, 375°F, Gas mark 5 for 15 minutes, then turn the heat down to 180°C, 350°F, Gas mark 4 and allow 25–30 minutes per 500g.

Roast Beef and Yorkshire Pudding

serves 6

a piece of sirloin or rib roast,
   or wing rib or forerib
salt and pepper
about 1 tablespoon plain flour
1 teaspoon mustard powder
about 300ml (10fl oz) beef stock

For the pudding
2 eggs, beaten
100g (4oz) plain flour, sifted
a pinch of salt
150ml (5fl oz) milk mixed with
   150ml (5fl oz) water
beef dripping from the roast

Take the beef out of the refrigerator about 1 hour before you want to start cooking it. Calculate the cooking time by the fast-roasting method (see page 23). Preheat the oven to 240°C, 475°F, Gas mark 9. Season a little flour with the mustard powder, salt and pepper and rub it into the fat. Put the meat, bones downward, into a suitable roasting tin and roast for 15 minutes, then reduce the heat to 180°C, 350°F, Gas mark 4.

While the meat is roasting, prepare the pudding batter. Mix the eggs, flour and salt. Then use a whisk to blend in the milk and water, to make a batter with the consistency of thin cream. Leave to stand.

After the beef has been removed from the oven to rest, turn up the heat to 220°C, 425°F, Gas mark 7. Add 1 generous tablespoon of dripping to the Yorkshire pudding tin and heat it in the oven until smoking hot. Pour in all but about 2 tablespoons of the batter (it should hiss spectacularly if the fat is at the right temperature), then return the pudding to the oven. Cook for about 30 minutes, until it is well browned in patches and light and crisp in texture.

To make the gravy, take the tin the beef was roasted in and spoon off any excess fat. Deglaze, preferably with stock. Let this bubble, and then, off the heat, stir in the remainder of the Yorkshire pudding batter, and keep stirring until the mixture thickens (you may need to heat it gently to achieve this). Add a little more stock if necessary, then taste and adjust the seasoning.

To follow tradition cut the pudding into squares and eat with gravy before the meat.

Slow-Roast Topside

Slow roasting is a good method for lean joints such as topside whose low fat content means they have a tendency to be dry.

serves 6

beef topside, 1.5–2kg (3½lb–4½lb)
extra beef fat, cut in thin slices
for barding (optional)

about 150ml (5fl oz) beef stock
about 1 tablespoon plain flour
salt and pepper

If you wish to bard the topside, arrange the fat in a layer over the meat and tie it on with string. Put the meat in a roasting tin that it fits reasonably well. Put in a low oven, 150°C, 300°F, Gas mark 2 (use the highest shelf in a gas oven) and allow 25 minutes per 500g for rare to medium-rare meat, 30–35 minutes for well done. About two-thirds of the way through cooking, season the meat with salt.

When the meat is cooked to your taste, remove it from the tin to a hot dish. Snip the strings holding the fat in place and discard them and the remains of the fat (the fat should have cooked through, so you may find it crisp and delicious). Keep the meat warm. Pour the cooking juices out of the roasting tin into a bowl, then deglaze the tin with a little stock and add this to the juices. Skim them, returning 2–3 tablespoons of fat to the roasting tin; stir in a little flour and allow it to cook and brown gently. Stir in the juices, plus stock as necessary, to make the gravy; taste and correct the seasoning, then serve.

Pot Roast Brisket of Beef

serves
6

2kg (4½lb) piece of rolled brisket
1 tablespoon olive oil
a handful of shallots, peeled
1 garlic clove, peeled and sliced
1 scant tablespoon plain flour
200ml (7fl oz) red wine
about 150ml (5fl oz) beef
   stock (optional)
1 teaspoon salt

For the marinade
2 teaspoons black peppercorns
2 blades of mace
6 cloves
fresh root ginger, about 1cm (½in)
   cube, peeled and finely grated
1 generous dessertspoon
   demerara sugar
1 garlic clove, peeled and crushed

To prepare the marinade, put the peppercorns, mace and cloves in a mortar and crush roughly. Stir in the ginger, sugar and garlic, then rub the beef with this mixture. Cover and leave overnight in a cool place or in the refrigerator.

To cook the meat, wipe the beef to remove most of the ground spices. Heat the oil in a casserole and cook the shallots and garlic briskly, stirring frequently, until they begin to brown slightly. Remove to a dish, then put the beef in the casserole and brown it all over. Then put the shallots and garlic around the meat, sprinkle over the flour and add the wine. It should cover the base of the casserole to a depth of about 2cm (¾in).

Fit a doubled sheet of greaseproof paper neatly across the top of the casserole, trimming so that it doesn't stick out and burn, then put the lid on over this. Cook very gently for 4 hours; this can be done on the lowest possible heat on top of the stove, or in a low oven at 140°C, 275°F, Gas mark 1. Check occasionally, especially if cooking on top of the stove, and add a little stock if necessary, as the gravy tends to reduce and catch; also, sprinkle the salt over the meat.

When cooked, remove the meat to a serving dish. Pour off the gravy and set it aside for a few minutes, then skim off the fat. You should be left with a glossy, deep-brown, rich-tasting sauce, which can be thinned with a little stock or water if you like. Check the seasoning. Slice the meat thinly, and pass round the gravy and some mashed potatoes (see page 210).

Shooter's Sandwich

serves 4

a piece of fillet steak from the 'tail' end,
  weighing about 500g (1lb 2oz)
2 tablespoons olive oil
100g (4oz) button mushrooms, sliced
15g (½oz) dried sliced porcini
  mushrooms (optional), soaked
  in 100ml (3½fl oz) warm water
  for 30 minutes – keep the soaking
  liquid
1 ciabatta loaf
salt

For the marinade
4 tablespoons red wine
2 teaspoons balsamic vinegar
1 garlic clove, peeled and crushed
1 dessertspoon finely chopped parsley
1 bay leaf, shredded
3–4 thyme sprigs, leaves only
3–4 marjoram sprigs, leaves only,
  chopped
2 tablespoons olive oil
freshly ground black pepper

Mix the marinade ingredients and put them into a shallow dish or bowl. Add the piece of fillet, rubbing well with the mixture, and leave to marinate, turning from time to time, for a minimum of 2 hours. It can be left for as long as 24 hours. Preheat the oven to 230°C, 450°F, Gas mark 8.

Heat the oil in a frying pan or a small, shallow cast-iron ovenproof dish. Add the sliced button mushrooms and fry briskly, stirring from time to time, until they begin to brown slightly at the edges. Stir in the soaked porcini and add their soaking liquid. If you have used a frying pan, transfer the mushroom mixture to an ovenproof dish at this point. Lift the beef out of the marinade, rubbing off any debris, and lay it on top of the mushrooms. Pour the marinade in underneath. Roast for 15–20 minutes. The meat should be rare to medium.

Slice the ciabatta in half lengthways and remove some of the crumb from each half, to leave a hollow into which the meat will fit. When the meat comes out of the oven, lay it in one side of the bread and distribute the mushroom mixture over it. The cooking liquid should have reduced to a few tablespoons (if it hasn't, reduce it by fast boiling). Pour the liquid over the meat and mushrooms. Season with a sprinkling of salt. Put on the top half of the loaf, pressing it down firmly to enclose the filling. Wrap firmly in foil, clingfilm or greaseproof paper. Put a small board on top and weight lightly with a couple of books or tins. Leave for 5–6 hours, then unwrap and cut across in slices at least 1cm (½in) thick.

Roast Veal with Sorrel Purée

A traditional combination lovely for a meal in late spring. Sorrel is not easy to obtain, but it is worth growing it or trying to buy some because it makes a delicious accompaniment for many things besides veal. For sorrel purée the relative amounts of sorrel and cream are fairly flexible.

serves 6

a piece of veal for roasting
    (topside, loin or chump)
    about 1.5–2kg (3½lb–4½lb)
30g (1oz) unsalted butter
1 scant teaspoon lemon zest
    (preferably unwaxed),
    finely grated
½ teaspoon black peppercorns,
    coarsely ground

1 fresh bay leaf – discard the central
    spine, and shred the leaf finely
salt

For the sorrel purée
15g (½oz) unsalted butter
100g (4oz) sorrel, washed and picked
    over – remove any tough stalks
150ml (5fl oz) double cream
salt and pepper

An hour or two before you want to cook the veal, soften the butter and mix in the lemon zest, pepper and bay leaf. Rub this mixture all over the meat and leave it, covered, in a cool place.

For cooking, select a roasting tin or casserole into which the meat will fit neatly, without too much space round the edges. Do not cover. Preheat the oven to 190°C, 375°F, Gas mark 5. Cook for 15–20 minutes, then reduce the heat to 180°C, 350°F, Gas mark 4 and continue to cook, basting with the juices from time to time. Salt lightly towards the end of cooking, and rest for 15 minutes.

Just before serving, make the sorrel purée. Melt the butter in a saucepan. Put in the sorrel, still damp but not wringing wet from washing, then stir over gentle heat until it collapses. The colour will change from a vivid green to a less attractive grey-brown, but don't let this worry you. As soon as it is all cooked, remove from the heat. Pour the cream into a clean pan and bring to the boil. Add the sorrel and cook gently for 2 minutes; add seasoning to taste.

Carve the meat in thin slices and spoon some of the buttery cooking juices over each plate. Serve with new potatoes and the sorrel purée.

Veal with Orange and Verjuice

The original idea for this came from a book first published in France by an author known simply as La Varenne. Translated into English as *The French Cook* (1653), it was an important text in the development of cookery techniques. This recipe uses verjuice (the juice of unripe apples or grapes), and it gives a pleasant fruity sourness without being overwhelming. If you can't get verjuice, use a not-too-dry white wine in this recipe.

serves 6

a piece of veal topside, about
    1.5kg (3½lb)
40g (1½oz) unsalted butter, softened
about 200ml (7fl oz) stock, preferably
    veal or chicken
about 1 tablespoon plain flour
salt

For the marinade
zest of 1 orange (preferably
    unwaxed), in thin strips
zest of ½ lemon (preferably
    unwaxed), in thin strips
6 tablespoons verjuice or wine
freshly ground black pepper

For the marinade, mix the orange and lemon zests with the verjuice and a little freshly ground pepper. Turn the veal in this mixture and leave to marinate for 5–6 hours, or overnight.

When you want to cook the meat, remove it from the marinade and scrape any bits of zest back into the marinade mixture.

Spread the butter over the meat, add a little salt, and put the meat in a roasting tin into which it fits reasonably well. Strain in the liquid from the marinade. Cook at 190°C, 375°F, Gas mark 5 for 15 minutes, then reduce the heat to 180°C, 350°F, Gas mark 4 and allow 25–30 minutes per 500g, basting frequently and adding a little stock to the tin if the juices show signs of drying up. About 15 minutes before the end of cooking time, add the zest from the marinade to the roasting tin (do not add it any earlier, or it will burn and blacken).

When the meat is done, remove it to a warmed serving dish and allow to rest. Pour the juices from the tin into a bowl. Deglaze the tin with a little stock, then add this to the juices. Spoon off excess fat, returning about 1 tablespoon of the liquid to the roasting tin, and sprinkle in a little flour. Stir over a low heat until it browns slightly, then stir in the cooking juices to make gravy.

Leftovers

BEEF IS ONE of the nicest meats to eat cold. A slice or two of it, slightly underdone, with a salad of green leaves and some potato salad, is excellent as a lunch or light evening meal for a hot day. It also makes good sandwiches (see below). Veal is less interesting when cold – the flavour becomes positively bland and the dryness is accentuated. British cookery has few solutions for what to do with the remains of a roast of veal.

Cold Roast Beef Sandwiches

serves
4

8 slices of bread, lightly buttered
4 dessertspoons mayonnaise
Horseradish Sauce, to taste

cold roast beef, sliced thinly
gherkins
salt and pepper

Lay out the pieces of bread destined to make the base of the sandwiches. Mix some mayonnaise (about 1 dessertspoon per sandwich, if using slices from a standard loaf) with a little horseradish to taste, and spread it over each slice. Distribute the beef over this, then season lightly, and add a few slices of pickled cucumber to each one. Complete with the remaining slices of bread.

serves
4

8 slices of bread, lightly buttered
4 dessertspoons mayonnaise
Dijon mustard, to taste

cold roast beef, sliced thinly
Crisp fried onions
salt and pepper

Proceed as above, but mix a little mustard into the mayonnaise instead of horseradish, and scatter the onions over the beef.

Bubble and Squeak

This can hardly be said to be a recipe: it is more a method for reheating various bits of leftover roast dinner. There are probably as many versions of bubble and squeak as there are people who make it. Originally a dish of fried cold beef, cabbage and potatoes appeared in recipes later in the 19th century (perhaps influenced by Irish colcannon) and other vegetables were sometimes added. In the mid-20th century, it was often served with sliced cold beef. Leftover cabbage and mashed potato, fried, remain the two vital ingredients. Aim for about half and half by volume of the two vegetables. The variety of cabbage may vary, but whatever is used, it must be well drained.

There are few rules in making bubble and squeak: the ingredients and their proportions depend to some extent on the contents of the larder. Adding fried onions or bits of fried bacon is entirely up to individual taste, as is the medium used for frying. Beef or pork fat left from a roast, or bacon dripping are all good. Butter burns too easily to work well with a potato-based version. Avoid oil, and fat from lamb or mutton.

Heat a frying pan and add a little fat – just enough to cover the base – and when hot, add the bubble and squeak mixture. Allow this to cook until the underside is nicely browned and crisp, then turn with a spatula. Don't worry if the 'cake' breaks up (one that keeps its shape is worryingly reminiscent of industrially produced versions), but continue to cook gently. Turning the mixture more during cooking evaporates some of the moisture and consolidates the mixture, although you will get a certain amount of the browned crust mixed into it.

Serve on its own, with cold beef, or reheated gravy, or as part of a breakfast fry-up.

Beef Ragù Made with Leftover Beef

A reasonable beef ragù (the type of sauce better known in English as Bolognese sauce) can be made with leftover roast beef. It won't be as good as one made with fresh beef, but provided it is made with care and good ingredients, it will be quite acceptable mixed through a bowl of pasta or used to stuff vegetables for baking, such as hollowed-out courgettes.

serves 4–6

30g (1oz) unsalted butter
60g (2½oz) unsmoked pancetta or lean bacon, finely chopped
1 medium onion, peeled and finely chopped
1 small carrot, coarsely grated
1 celery stick, washed and finely chopped
2 large mushrooms, washed and finely chopped
2 garlic cloves, peeled and crushed

250g (9oz) cold roast beef, trimmed of fat, gristle and outside bits, and minced
150–200ml (5–7fl oz) red wine
100–150g (4–5oz) passata (bottled sieved tomatoes)
1 bay leaf (optional)
a pinch of dried thyme (optional)
a pinch of dried marjoram (optional)
scant 1 teaspoon salt
freshly ground black pepper

Melt the butter in a large frying pan or flameproof casserole and fry the pancetta until the fat is translucent. Add the onion and cook over low heat until it begins to soften. Add the carrot, celery, mushrooms and garlic, and continue to cook, stirring from time to time, until the vegetables begin to soften and brown. Add the beef and stir in well, then pour in the wine and allow it to bubble. Stir in the passata and the herbs, if using, and finally season with the salt and grind in some pepper. Simmer very gently for about 1 hour. Taste and correct the seasoning.

Cold Beef, Hashed

The standard English method for re-presenting leftover beef (or any other meat) was to make it into a hash – cutting the meat up small, making a sauce to reheat it with, and adding flavourings as taste and imagination dictated. 'There is not any Thing in which the Cook may so much indulge her Fancy as in a Hash; for almost any Thing may be put into it', wrote Martha Bradley in 1756. This is Alexis Soyer's 'Hashed Beef Another Way', which works well with small amounts of beef to make a dish for one or two people.

serves
1 or 2

15g (½oz) unsalted butter
1 tablespoon finely chopped onion
50g (2oz) sliced mushrooms (optional)
75–100g (3–4oz) cold roast beef, cut
    into small thin slices
1 dessertspoon plain flour mixed with
    a little salt and pepper

150ml (5fl oz) beef stock
1–2 pickled gherkins, sliced
some vinegar from the gherkins
1 teaspoon chopped parsley or
    tarragon (optional)
walnut ketchup, to taste (optional)
salt and pepper

Melt the butter in a frying pan. Add the onion and cook briskly, stirring frequently, until lightly browned. Add the mushrooms, if using.

Toss the slices of meat with the seasoned flour, then add them to the onion and turn them in the pan to warm through. Add the stock plus the gherkins and a little of their preserving vinegar (don't overdo this; you can always add a little more towards the end). Bring to a simmer, then taste and add more seasoning if desired. If using the chopped herbs or walnut ketchup, add these at the end as well.

Beef and Vegetable Broth

serves
4

1 litre (1¾ pints) good beef stock
¼ medium-sized turnip or swede,
    washed and peeled
1 leek, washed and trimmed
3 celery sticks, washed and trimmed

a few leaves of curly
    kale, washed
2 large carrots, washed,
    trimmed and peeled
salt and pepper

Put the stock in a pan (one that will go in the oven is a good idea, or use a slow cooker) and bring to the boil. While it heats, chop all the vegetables finely and add them to the pan. Stir in 1 teaspoon salt. Cover, and when it boils, transfer to a low oven or a slow cooker and leave to cook. It should be ready after about 1½ hours.

The fresher the vegetables, the better the soup will be. Finely chopped celeriac or kohlrabi, or a tomato, skinned and chopped, are all good additions.

Eliza Acton's Veal Loaf

Eliza Acton gave this recipe under the name of 'Bordyke veal cake' (Bordyke was the street in Tonbridge where she lived). It is intended for fresh veal but works quite well with the remains of a roast, and it makes a meatloaf like a close-textured, coarse pâté.

serves
6–8

700g (1½lb) cold roast veal,
    free from bones, fat and gristle
225g (8oz) unsmoked streaky bacon
2 medium eggs, lightly beaten
zest of 1 lemon (preferably unwaxed)

a generous pinch of cayenne pepper
a pinch of grated nutmeg
½ teaspoon ground mace
½ teaspoon salt
unsalted butter, for greasing

Preheat the oven to 180°C, 350°F, Gas mark 4. Mince or chop the veal and bacon together thoroughly. Mix in the eggs, lemon zest and all the seasonings. Grease a round ovenproof dish and pack in the meat mixture. Cover the surface with foil or buttered greaseproof paper. Bake for 1–1¼ hours. Smaller amounts can be packed in individual ramekin dishes, which need about 25 minutes baking.

Eat hot with a light tomato sauce, or cold with salad and new potatoes.

Lamb & Mutton

LAMB AND MUTTON both refer to the meat of sheep, but there is an age distinction, and – unless you are a shepherd or a butcher – the terminology can be confusing. Alive, a sheep is considered a lamb from birth in the spring until the turn of the year. For the next 12 months, the animal becomes a hoggett, and after that it is a sheep.

As meat, lambs may be killed at about 10–12 weeks old for Easter, but most reach the market at between 5 and 12 months (still called lamb, and probably what 19th-century authors referred to as 'grass-fed lamb'). Then it enters a kind of culinary no man's land, when it is really mutton, but mutton that is too young to have acquired flavour or character. After its second winter, the meat will taste more interesting, especially if grazed on some distinctive species-rich grassland or hill pasture. The full flavour develops at around 3 years old, but to be really good, according to judges in past centuries, the best mutton came from animals 5 or even 6 years old, and wethers – castrated rams – were thought to give the best meat.

Five-year-old wether mutton was always difficult to obtain, and is impossible to buy these days. The prices for wool (which gave live sheep added value) fell, and keeping animals beyond the age at which they can first be sold is uneconomic because of the feed required. Mutton seems to have lost favour some time shortly after the end of World War II, and is only just starting to come back, slowly, into fashion. Our ancestors ate a lot of mutton, some of it very fatty and coarse, which is probably why the market for it declined when ample supplies of frozen New Zealand lamb became available.

Until the mid-19th century, there was a certain amount of 'house lamb' production, indoor rearing of out-of-season young lambs. These animals, which had pale, tender flesh but not much flavour, were a luxury for Christmas, eaten young.

Lamb, in the sense in which we now understand it, is more seasonal than beef: it is usually born between January and May in the British Isles. We've completely lost sucking lamb, but new season's lamb is sought-after for Easter, when the home-bred item will just be coming on to the market (some farmers lamb around Christmas specifically to supply the Easter market). The bulk of it becomes available in the late spring and early summer, running through to September or October. This is the point when lowland animals are getting towards being hoggetts. As the autumn progresses, good mutton becomes a better option than overgrown lamb – if you can buy it.

Lamb and mutton, when it arrived before the roasting range in kitchens of the past, was, like beef, sometimes regarded as too good to be messed around with. The best mutton was simply roasted, as was young house lamb. A favourite combination in English cookery books during the 17th and 18th centuries was mutton with oysters – cheap and easily available, these were mixed into stuffings, rolled in spice and herb mixtures and used to lard the meat, or added to the sauce. The dish went out of fashion in the second half of the 19th century, when oyster beds around the British coast were ruined by pollution, disease and bad weather and the shellfish became an expensive luxury. Another dish involved hollowing out the lean meat from a partly roasted joint – in this case, from the inside of the leg – then chopping and pounding the meat with flavourings, and stuffing it back in the cavity and returning it to roast. The meat off a shoulder, roasted until almost done, was also sometimes taken off the bone, and the meat cut away from the inside and hashed (from the French *hacher*, to chop or mince). The bones and outer layer were grilled and served on top of the hash, a dish sometimes called 'Shoulder of Mutton in Epigram'.

Other cuts included chine and saddle. Chine was two best ends and the backbone in between, and it seems to have gone out of favour by the end of the 18th century. A saddle was both the loins, with the chump part of the rump attached; sometimes the kidneys (located under the loin) were taken out, each wrapped in a 'tail' of fat from the rear end of the saddle, and skewered to it as decorative full stops. This joint was regarded as suitable for large formal parties, and it appears in the novels of John Galsworthy on the table at Forsyte family gatherings – symbolic, perhaps, of stuffy upper-middle-class conservatism. Like a baron of beef, this particular joint has vanished into history because of legislation relating to the dressing of sheep for sale as meat. A saddle of lamb can still be purchased, though you might have to order it.

We tend to forget that lamb was much anticipated as a meat for the early summer, and considered to go best with summer vegetables – peas, new potatoes and small turnips. Mint sauce fitted in with this general summer scheme. In the 18th century, cucumber-based dishes were often served with mutton, while the 19th-century preference was for redcurrant jelly or onion sauce. Stuffing was sometimes used with meat from sheep, more to soak up fat than to add it.

British cookery has a persistent thread of serving lamb or mutton with flavours derived from the sea. Laverbread is one such example, as is samphire (plainly cooked, and served as a vegetable accompaniment, or cut into short lengths and stirred into the gravy). Fish flavours such as oysters or anchovy (much used in the late 17th and early 18th centuries) are also found in many recipes and go surprisingly well with the meat, more so if you can source a piece of saltmarsh-grazed meat.

During the second half of the 20th century, cookery writers began to introduce ideas from the peasant and country kitchens of southern Europe and the Middle East. Strong herb flavours and the use of fruit with lamb or mutton reappeared in English cookery after an absence of about four centuries. The idea of larding a leg of lamb with slivers of garlic and sprigs of rosemary, or concocting a rice and apricot stuffing, both come from this interest in Mediterranean traditions.

Buying Lamb and Mutton and Cuts for Roasting

Butchers often identify where their lamb comes from. As always, the ideal supplier will know the farmers who rear the animals and will be able to tell you about the produce.

Lamb should hang for 7–10 days. Mutton can hang for longer; 19th-century cooks considered that it should hang for as long as possible. Look for firm, dull red lean meat in lamb and dull brownish-red in mutton, with hard white fat and small bones. Avoid excessive fat. Mutton can be difficult to buy, but a good butcher may be able to source it.

Sheep are cut into fore- and hindquarters. The hindquarter includes the leg (known in Scotland as the gigot, pronounced 'jiggot'), a favourite roasting joint that weighs 2–3.5kg (4½–7¾lb), depending on the breed and age of the animal. It is usually possible to buy a half leg, which means you have to choose between a round piece of lean, or a longer, slimmer shank end, with smaller muscles, but sweeter meat. The loin (which together with the leg makes a haunch) is also a good roasting joint, but since it is usually cut into chops, this has to be ordered. Equally, you are unlikely to be able to buy a haunch except by special request.

The forequarter includes the 'best end', or rack of lamb. This is a very good small roasting joint, with a neat appearance when nicely trimmed; make sure it is chined and that the long bones are divided at the joints to make it easy to separate them. The shoulder contains the bladebone and the long bone adjoining it, plus a knuckle. Bonier and fattier than leg, it is a good roasting joint with a sweeter flavour, and is cheaper. A whole shoulder will generally weigh 2–2.5kg (4½–5½lb), up to 3–3.5kg (6½–7¾lb) for mutton, but it is often sold cut diagonally in half. Finally, the breast – a cut taken from the ends of the ribs – can also be used for roasting. It tends to be chewy, as it contains thin sheets of muscle interspersed with connective tissue, and is also fatty, but has a good flavour and is very inexpensive.

As with beef, the question of rare or well done is really down to personal preference. For those who are undecided, leg and best end are probably both better cooked on the rare side, but shoulder benefits from being fully cooked – this will cook out some of the fat and crisp up the skin.

For individual recipes, I have given specific temperatures and approximate times, but if all you want is a plain roast joint of lamb or mutton, times and temperatures for fast roasting are similar to those for beef, although I would start it at a slightly lower temperature:

• For a fast roast, give the meat 20 minutes at 220°C, 425°F, Gas mark 7, then reduce the heat to 180°C, 350°F, Gas mark 4 and cook for the following times:
  Lamb or mutton on the bone: 15 minutes per 500g (rare); 18–20 minutes per 500g (medium); 25 minutes per 500g (well done). Boneless: 12 minutes per 500g (rare); 13–15 minutes per 500g (medium); 20 minutes per 500g (well done).

• For slow roasting, which works well with leg of mutton, cook at 150°C, 300°F, Gas mark 2 for the entire time, allowing 60 minutes per 500g.

• For breast of lamb or mutton, see recipe on page 46.

Roast Leg of Mutton with Anchovies and Orange Peel

3kg (6½lb) leg of mutton, bone in
1 tablespoon olive oil
2 large garlic cloves, peeled and each
   cut into 2–3 chunks
1 large shallot, peeled and quartered
1 bay leaf (optional)
some fresh marjoram sprigs (optional)
200ml (7fl oz) red wine
200ml (7fl oz) well-flavoured stock
2 tablespoons plain flour

freshly ground black pepper
½ teaspoon salt

For the larding

8–10 anchovy fillets preserved in oil,
   drained
1 large orange (preferably unwaxed)
18–20 fresh rosemary sprigs,
   about 3cm (1¼in) long

Cut the anchovy fillets into strips about 2cm (¾in) long and 5mm (¼in) wide. Pare the zest from the orange to make about 20–25 strips of zest. Keep the orange – you'll need the juice later.

Take the mutton and use a sharp knife to make parallel rows of small incisions, about 4cm (1½in) apart, from the broad end to the shank. Make a row, with rosemary sprigs in each incision; in the second row, pieces of anchovy; in the third, slivers of orange zest. Repeat until the larding ingredients have been used up.

Put the olive oil in a roasting tin. Add the garlic and shallot, the bay leaf and the marjoram. Sit the meat on top and sprinkle with salt. Cook at 170°C, 325°F, Gas mark 3 for about 2 hours, then pour the red wine and the juice of the orange into the roasting tin and return to roast for a further 1½ hours, until the juices run clear. Put the joint on a warm plate, cover loosely with foil, and leave to rest.

Pour the cooking juices into a bowl. Put the roasting tin over a low heat. Stir in half the stock, scraping the tin to incorporate all the residue, and add to the reserved juices. Return the tin to the heat and add 2–3 tablespoons of the meat fat. Stir in the flour and allow to brown lightly. Skim any fat off the cooking juices. Strain these into the tin, stirring, and bring to the boil to make a lightly thickened gravy. Add the remainder of the stock, taste, and check the seasoning.

Shoulder of Mutton
with or without Oysters

serves 6

1 shoulder of mutton, 2–2.5kg
  (4½–5½lb), boned weight
1 tablespoon finely chopped fresh
  marjoram
zest of 1 lemon (preferably unwaxed),
  grated
a pinch of freshly grated nutmeg

250ml (9fl oz) dry white wine
12 oysters (optional)
1 small shallot, peeled and finely
  chopped
1 tablespoon plain flour
stock or water, to taste
½ teaspoon salt

If the butcher has rolled and tied the meat, cut the string and unroll it to expose the inside. Scatter over the marjoram, lemon zest, a generous grating of nutmeg and the salt. Re-roll and tie firmly.

Preheat the oven to 220°C, 425°F, Gas mark 7. To calculate the cooking time, see page 46. Put the meat into a roasting tin and cook for about 30 minutes. Baste with the wine, sprinkle the surface of the meat with salt, and reduce the heat to 180°C, 350°F, Gas mark 4. Continue to cook until done to your taste. Baste with the cooking juices at intervals.

When the meat is done, remove to a warmed serving plate and leave to rest. Pour all the roasting juices out of the tin into a bowl and allow the fat to rise; skim off as much as possible and reserve.

If using, open the oysters, strain their liquor through a sieve lined with kitchen paper to catch any bits of shell or sand, and reserve in a separate bowl.

Add about 2 tablespoons of the fat back to the roasting tin, heat gently and cook the chopped shallot in it until translucent. Add the flour and continue stirring and cooking until lightly browned. Stir in the roasting juices to make a smooth gravy. If using oysters, add their liquor at this point, stirring, and bring to a simmer. Just before serving, stir in the oysters and continue to cook gently for a few minutes. They must be thoroughly hot. Otherwise, proceed as for a conventional gravy, adding a little stock and adjusting the seasoning to taste.

Rack of Lamb with a Herb Crust

The rack, or best end of neck of lamb, consists of 6–8 cutlets joined together, and must be chined. Often the ends of the bones are cleaned of all meat, and sometimes decorated with paper frills. Two racks presented with the bones making a crisscross formation are known as a guard of honour; three, curved and stitched together vertically so that the meat is inside and the bones radiate in a sunburst, is a crown roast, which was very fashionable during the 1970s. A lone rack of lamb is a good joint for 2–3 people (although don't expect leftovers), and also one that is nice cold.

serves 2–3

1 rack of lamb, trimmed
1 fresh rosemary sprig
30g (1oz) fresh white breadcrumbs
2 tablespoons chopped parsley
1 tablespoon chopped basil
1 garlic clove, peeled and crushed
½ teaspoon salt

Preheat the oven to 180°C, 350°F, Gas mark 4.

Remove the parchment-like skin covering the meat (a thin layer of fat should remain) and scrape the bones if the butcher hasn't done this for you. Put the lamb, bones down, in a small roasting tin or ovenproof dish, tucking the rosemary underneath. Roast for 30–40 minutes, depending on the size of the rack.

While the lamb cooks, mix the breadcrumbs, parsley, basil, garlic and salt. After the initial roasting, remove the meat from the oven and turn up the heat to 200°C, 400°F, Gas mark 6. Carefully spread the breadcrumb and herb mixture over the fat layer, pressing it down well. Roast for another 10 minutes.

This roast does not produce any gravy worth speaking of, so if you wish to serve it hot, good accompaniments are those which add moisture, such as Boulangère Potatoes (see page133) or a dish of baked tomatoes.

Slow-Roast Mutton and Salsa Verde

This recipe was originally created for Herdwick mutton; these sheep, born with black pelts that turn grey or rusty brown as they grow, have distinctive pale heads, small curved horns, and are principally found on the highest of the Lake District fells. Meat from other breeds will work equally well, although try to acquire mutton rather than lamb. Salsa verde, which includes both capers and mint, recalls the English traditions of caper sauce with mutton and mint sauce with lamb.

serves 6–8

a whole leg of mutton, bone in salt

For the salsa verde
a good handful each of fresh mint,
  parsley and basil
1 small garlic clove, peeled and
  crushed
2 tablespoons capers, rinsed of any salt
  or vinegar in which they have been
  preserved
2 tablespoons Dijon mustard
2 tablespoons red wine vinegar
8 tablespoons olive oil

Salt the meat lightly and cook in a very low oven, 140°C, 275°F, Gas mark 1, allowing 60 minutes per 500g.

To make the salsa verde, wash the herbs and pick off the leaves, discarding the stalks. Blend all the ingredients together, taste and season.

Carve the mutton and serve the sauce separately.

Breast of Lamb Stuffed with Capers, Garlic and Herbs

serves 3–4

2 breasts of lamb, boned
40g (1½oz) unsalted butter
1 medium onion, peeled and finely
　chopped
2 garlic cloves, peeled and crushed
2 tablespoons salted capers, well rinsed
　and coarsely chopped
a little chopped fresh mint

3 tablespoons finely chopped fresh
　parsley
large tablespoon chopped fresh basil
zest of ½ lemon (preferably unwaxed),
　finely grated
150g (5oz) crustless day-old white
　bread, torn into small pieces
splash of stock or milk, to moisten

Breast of lamb is flattish and thin, with one straight edge cut from the forequarter, which may still contain the ends of the rib bones, unless the butcher has already removed them. If you have to do this yourself, run a knife in between the bones and the meat on the outside, then cut them away from the lesser covering inside and slip them out.

To make the stuffing, melt the butter over a low heat and fry the onion and garlic until softened. Stir in the capers, herbs, lemon zest and bread, and add enough stock or milk to moisten the bread.

Spread the meat out, skin side down. Put a layer of stuffing on top of each piece, then roll from the narrow end and tie at each end with string – firmly, but not so tight that all the stuffing oozes out.

Preheat the oven to 140°C, 275°F, Gas mark 1. Put the lamb in a shallow roasting tin and cook for 3–3½ hours, pouring off any fat that the meat renders. Then turn the oven up to 200°C, 400°F, Gas mark 6, and give it a further 15 minutes to crisp up.

It will not produce gravy, but a light tomato sauce goes well with the caper-flavoured stuffing. Alternatively, serve a salad dressed with vinaigrette on the side.

Dried Apricot and Almond Stuffing

While lamb or mutton cooked on the bone scores best for flavour, it is not the easiest thing to carve. Both leg and shoulder are often boned, creating joints ideal for stuffing. This recipe uses a fruit and nut combination derived from Arab cookery. Stuff the joint, then roll and tie with string. Or, if using a boned shoulder, tie it as a 'cushion' – in four, like a parcel – or as a 'melon' – manoeuvre the stuffed meat into a rough ball shape, then take a long piece of string and wrap it four times round the meat, crossing at the poles, giving the appearance of eight sections like a cantaloupe melon. Carve a rolled joint into slices, and a cushion or melon into sections.

serves 3–4

40g (1½oz) unsalted butter
1 small onion, peeled and very finely chopped
50g (2oz) almonds, blanched and cut into slivers
150g (5oz) crustless day-old white bread, torn into small pieces
75g (3oz) dried apricots, soaked for a few hours, then drained and chopped roughly

zest of ½ lemon (preferably unwaxed), finely grated
a generous pinch of freshly grated nutmeg
50–100ml (2–3½fl oz) stock or milk
½ teaspoon salt
freshly ground black pepper

Melt the butter in a small frying pan and sauté the onion gently until translucent. Toast the almonds lightly in the oven for 5–10 minutes; watch to make sure they don't burn. In a bowl, combine the onion, almonds, bread, apricots and lemon zest. Season with a generous grating of nutmeg, the salt and some pepper. Mix well and pour in just enough stock or milk to make the bread moist but not soggy.

Use to stuff the cavity left by boning the joint and roast. To calculate the cooking time, see page 46. Alternatively, make into small balls and bake in a lightly greased dish for about 20–30 minutes at 180°C, 350°F, Gas mark 4.

Laver Sauce

serves
4

75g (3oz) unsalted butter
450g (1lb) prepared laverbread
juice of 1 Seville orange
salt and pepper

Melt the butter in a saucepan, add the laverbread, and stir gently until hot. Squeeze in the orange juice. Taste and adjust the seasoning with a little salt and pepper if you consider it necessary.

If Seville oranges are unobtainable, use a mixture of lemon juice and sweet orange juice instead.

Cucumber Chutney

serves
3–4

5cm (2in) length of cucumber
a pinch of granulated sugar
1 dessertspoon white wine vinegar
about 1 tablespoon finely chopped
 herbs – a combination of two
 or more of the following: chives,
 parsley, coriander, mint

a small piece of fresh hot green chilli
 pepper (or to taste), finely chopped
1 dessertspoon olive oil
salt and pepper

Peel the cucumber and cut in half crossways, then cut both pieces into slim julienne strips. Dissolve the sugar in the vinegar and pour over the cucumber. Stir in the chopped herbs, chilli pepper and olive oil. Season to taste.

Serve with slices of cold roast lamb or mutton and a salad of bitter leaves, lightly dressed with lemon juice and olive oil.

Mint Sauce

By the mid-20th century, mint sauce seemed to be the preferred accompaniment for lamb, combining two elements that go well with this meat – a strongly aromatic perfume and a sharp taste. Unfortunately, it was often badly made. For mint sauce lovers, Eliza Acton's recipe of 3 heaped teaspoons of finely chopped young fresh mint, 2 heaped teaspoons of caster sugar and 6 teaspoons of 'the best vinegar' (try a good white wine one) is a good formula. Stir together until the sugar has dissolved.

Leftovers

Shepherd's (or Cottage) Pie

This dish, a standard method for using up leftover roast lamb or mutton, seems to have first appeared in the 1870s, when mincing machines were developed. Cottage pie is the name usually given to a beef version. This is a basic recipe for either beef or lamb.

serves 4

1 tablespoon fat from the roast, or oil
1 large onion, peeled and finely chopped
1 garlic clove, peeled and crushed
450–500g (1–1lb 2oz) cold roast meat
    (remove any skin, gristle, most of
    the fat and any bits of herbs left
    over from roasting)
300ml (10fl oz) leftover gravy, plus a
    little stock

about 1 tablespoon chopped parsley
salt and pepper

For the topping
1kg (2¼lb) floury potatoes
200ml (7fl oz) milk
30–40g (1–1½oz) unsalted butter
salt and pepper

Heat the fat in a large frying pan and add the onion and garlic. Let it cook gently without browning for 10–15 minutes. Chop the meat finely, or put it through a mincing machine (this produces a softer texture). Add the meat to the pan with the onion. Stir well and add the gravy, plus a little stock (or water) if the mixture seems dry. Taste for seasoning, adding salt and pepper as necessary, then add some chopped parsley. Lightly grease an ovenproof dish and pour in the meat mixture. For the topping, peel the potatoes, chop roughly and boil until just tender. Drain and mash with the milk, butter, salt and pepper.

Preheat the oven to 190°C, 375°F, Gas mark 5. Cover the meat with the mashed potato, roughening the surface with a fork. Brown in the oven for about 30 minutes, or leave to go cold and reheat (same temperature).

If you are cooking the beef version, Cottage Pie, try stirring 2–3 teaspoons of truffle oil into the mashed potato and sprinkle the top with grated cheese, such as strong Cheddar or Parmesan. Cook as above.

Scotch Broth

Stock from lamb or mutton bones has a distinctive flavour, best used with robust vegetable combinations found in the Scotch Broth tradition.

serves
4

1 litre (1¾ pints) stock made with the
    bones from a lamb or mutton roast
40g (1½oz) split peas (yellow or green),
    soaked overnight
40g (1½oz) pearl barley
2 medium carrots, scraped and sliced
1 small turnip, about 75g (3oz), peeled
    and chopped
1 leek, cleaned, trimmed and chopped

1 celery stick, washed and chopped
a few leaves of curly kale, washed and
    shredded
salt and pepper
chopped parsley

Put the stock in a pan and add the soaked split peas, barley and all the vegetables except the kale. Simmer gently until the peas and barley are soft. Add the kale and cook for about 10 minutes longer. Check the seasoning and add salt and pepper as needed.

Divide the broth between bowls and add parsley just before serving.

Pilaf

I first encountered the idea of a pilaf in Elizabeth David's *Mediterranean Food* (1950), although lamb and rice dishes appear in English cookery books as early as the 17th century. It's a good method for stretching a small amount of leftover meat, or using up an odd slice or two in a dish for one person. Ingredients and quantities depend to some extent on the contents of the refrigerator and your appetite: the following are suggestions.

serves
4

75–100g (3–4oz) long-grain rice
1 tablespoon pine nuts or blanched
    almonds, cut into slivers
1 tablespoon olive oil
¼–½ medium onion, peeled and
    chopped
1 garlic clove, peeled and sliced
75g (3oz) cooked mutton or lamb, cut
    into small chunks, with any skin,
    gristle and large pieces of fat removed

about 1 tablespoon raisins and
    currants, mixed
1 large ripe tomato, skinned and
    sliced, or 1–2 tablespoons
    passata (bottled sieved tomatoes)
salt and pepper

Boil the rice according to your favourite method.

Toast the nuts lightly in a heated frying pan, then set aside. Add the oil to the pan and fry the onion gently. Add the garlic, and continue to cook until the onion is translucent. Add the meat, and continue to fry gently. Add the raisins and currants, and keep stirring; after a moment, add the nuts. Finally, stir in the tomato or passata.

By now, the rice should be cooked. Drain if necessary and stir in the meat mixture. Leave covered for a few minutes, then serve with natural yoghurt or Cucumber Chutney (see page 58). Some Crisp Fried Browned Onions (see page 220) make a good garnish, or add 1 tablespoon chopped parsley.

Pilaf stuffing

To make a stuffing, use 200g (7oz) rice, and omit the meat and tomato. Use butter in place of the oil, and add pine nuts, currants and chopped parsley to flavour, or almonds and apricots.

Pork, Ham & Gammon

PORK COMES FROM PORKERS. This may seem a statement of the obvious, but pigs are graded by age and weight. A porker is a relatively young pig, which has achieved the optimum weight for fresh meat but is not large enough for salting for bacon and ham (for that, one needs, naturally, a baconer). Pigs for fresh pork can be grown on to be older and heavier, but as with all animal rearing, the economics of feed versus the return on the meat come into play. In some cultures, pork is taboo, but to the poor of the British Isles, and much of Europe, it often provided the small amount of meat they ate for most of the year. Pigs breed fast and have large litters, and a piglet could be acquired for relatively little money. In towns, they were fed on household scraps and what they could scavenge in the street (in spite of the authorities' attempts to control them, pigs were a common sight in the streets of many towns until the early 18th century).

In the countryside they might have been confined in a sty, or allowed a freer range (although pannage, the autumn feeding of pigs on acorns and beechmast in woodland, seems to have declined after the Middle Ages). They had their place, too, in the wider rural economy, especially in cheese-making areas, where they consumed the whey left over from this process. In short, these were useful animals, quick providers of meat in restricted space, for relatively little outlay.

This does not mean that the rural poor ate roast pork every Sunday. For a start, fresh pork was considered dangerous in summer, well into the 19th century. The meat does not keep well in hot weather, and effective refrigeration did not develop until the 1880s. Pigs were killed only during the cooler months of the year – the rule of thumb being only when there is an 'r' in the month (like oysters). In addition, most of the meat was salted for hams and bacon. These were stored and used slowly throughout the year, until the next pig was ready for the kill, although the hams were often sold to pay various household expenses, including the acquisition of the next piglet.

The fresh pork that the poor got under this system was usually the offcuts from baconers. The better-off, who could afford to buy meat, might acquire the cuts we are familiar with, but recipes for roasting pork in British culinary traditions are few and mostly simple. Favourite cuts seem to have been leg of pork and griskin – the lean part of the loin.

In the mid-19th century, Eliza Acton observed of roast pork that it 'is not at the present day much served at very good tables, particularly in this form', which may have reflected a general and longstanding feeling that it was not the most elegant of meats. She also commented on the 'old savoury stuffing of sage and onions', showing that this combination – still the one that springs most readily to mind when roast pork and English culinary traditions are mentioned – was considered a tradition even then.

Sucking pig was a different matter – special food. It was uneconomic to kill such a young and potentially productive animal for food (they were considered best at 3–4 weeks old). However, in communities whose ability to store fresh meat was limited but which had ready access to live animals, a sucking pig represented a luxury meal on the hoof. Given that a sow can have two or three litters a year, and breeds all year round, there was always likely to be one such pig available – and it could be cooked as soon as it was dressed (in 1756, Martha Bradley said it was best killed on the morning of the day it was to be cooked). Properly roasted, it provided an exquisite combination of tender, mildly flavoured meat with delicately crisp skin – and as with all relatively large and spectacular pieces of meat, it had extra status.

Roasting a sucking pig in front of an open fire required a great deal of attention to make sure the entire animal cooked evenly. They are long, and made even longer by the habit of trussing them with their front legs forward and hind legs back, thus requiring a fireplace that was also long. There was also the possibility that the plumper mid-section, closer to the fire than the slender little trotters, would be cooked through and scorching while the extremities were still raw. To counteract this, a special shield known as a pig-iron was sometimes suspended from the fire grate to lessen the heat received by the pig's midriff.

Of the meat that was salted, most bacon was used in the form of rashers to flavour other foods, and was enjoyed by both rich and poor. Hams, though, were a high-status item, which might be cooked whole to make an appearance on the tables of the wealthy. Usually they were boiled, but roasting and baking were alternative cooking methods, and were sometimes preferred to boiling. Both gammon and ham refer to the hind leg of a pig above the hock joint, cured by salting and drying, but there seems to have been a distinction in the past: a ham was cured as a separate piece of meat, whereas a gammon seems to have been left attached to a bacon flitch and cured as part of the side – a trickier process because of the varying thicknesses of meat involved. The words now seem to be used more or less interchangeably, although gammon sometimes implies a milder cure.

Buying Pork

Pork, like beef and lamb, has been bred for lean meat over the past 30–40 years. Pork that is very lean is dull in flavour and dry in texture. On the other hand, no one wants to pay for large amounts of fat. To produce really good pork, as with other meat, a balance has to be struck. Tradition – a breed that might have decorated the apple orchards of the south-west, or have been a talisman to a thrifty cottager – conflicts with the economics of bringing an animal to the optimum weight for meat in the shortest possible time with the highest proportion of lean and desirable prime meat. Pragmatism usually wins, and lean commercial stock is used for porkers, but this will not be very flavoursome. Some butchers make a point of sourcing traditional and rare breed meat from slightly older animals, because the slower growth means more flavour. What the pig eats also makes a difference, both to flavour and to the texture of the fat.

Another factor in the flavour of pork is something called 'boar taint'. While male cattle and some sheep destined for meat are castrated, in Britain, male pigs are left intact, and this can lead to a distinctive flavour in the meat. Musky is a polite way to describe it. The issues behind this relate both to animal welfare and commercial implications to do with the way the animal gains weight. The theory is that taint will not be a problem since pigs are slaughtered for pork before puberty (when boar taint develops, as a result of hormonal changes). However, other factors operate: some pigs have more of the flavour, or enter puberty at a younger than average age, while some people are more sensitive to the flavour. The only way to counter this problem is to know your supplier, and to avoid the problem entirely you will either have to buy meat from female pigs, or find a supplier who castrates the males (important for traditional breeds that are grown on to be older than average).

When buying pork, look for lean meat that is pale pink, moist but firm; the fat should be white, firm but tender and present in reasonable but not excessive amounts. To store, remove shop wrappings, cover loosely and place on a plate or tray in the coolest part of the refrigerator.

Cuts for Roasting and Roasting Times

Because the lean is tender and the fat usually ample, most cuts of pork are suitable for roasting. The loin and leg contain the highest proportion of lean meat in large muscles. A whole leg of pork is a big joint that tends to be dry if not carefully cooked. Forequarter cuts tend to be fattier and have more connective tissue, but they still roast well, especially slowly. If it's crackling that you want, choose a piece of loin, a joint fairly even in shape along its entire length; it can produce spectacular results. Loin, as with other animals, has a long tender undercut (often sold separately as fillet); if you are fortunate, it will be left in place, an extra treat.

Most people would consider removing the skin to be a waste, but if you want a less fatty result, or to marinate the meat, this is a necessity. The skin on all pork joints should be scored, to help it crisp, and to divide it after cooking – most butchers will do this for you

Stuffing, including that old-fashioned mixture of sage and onion, is sometimes used for flavour and to counteract dryness in cuts such as leg. Other flavourings for pork tend to fall into three categories: fruity, aromatic and sweet. In Britain, apple sauce or baked apples provide the former and are especially good with a really well-produced traditional-breed meat, the sweetness of the apple picking up on the inherent sweet note of well-fed pork. Lemon zest is also a good flavouring for pork, especially with rosemary, thyme, fennel, garlic and black pepper. Chinese culture has provided a different range of flavourings, especially star anise, five-spice powder, and soy sauce in combinations with sugar or honey. These go particularly well with slow-roast pork.

Pork should always be thoroughly cooked. A rule of thumb for all cuts is to start the meat at 230°C, 450°F, Gas mark 8 for 20 minutes, then reduce the heat to 170°C, 325°F, Gas mark 3 and allow 25 minutes per 500g for prime cuts (leg, loin) or 30 minutes per 500g for other cuts. I prefer to cook belly pork and forequarter cuts on slow, 140°C, 275°F, Gas mark 1 for 60 minutes per 500g. A meat thermometer is especially useful when cooking ham or gammon. Because these are cured meats, they remain pink even when fully cooked, and it is less easy to tell when they are done.

Crackling

How to get crackling to crackle is, to some extent, a matter of knowing your oven and working out the optimum time and temperature. Slow roasting is a more reliable way of producing crackling than fast roasting, simply because it gives the skin longer to crisp up and is less likely to scorch the edges of the joint. A method frequently recommended – at least since the 19th century – is to rub the skin of pork with olive oil and salt before cooking.

Whatever method is used, three points help to provide good results. The first is that the meat must have a reasonable covering of fat: look for a layer just over 1cm (½in) thick, certainly not less. The next is that the skin should be properly scored; this needs to be done neatly in parallel lines at intervals of about 1cm (½in) apart, to about the same depth. The cuts might go down to the lean, but should not penetrate it. A good butcher will usually ask about this. The third point is that the skin should be dry when the meat is put into the oven. This makes the following method, derived from Chinese cookery, seem rather strange, but it does work:

• Put the pork, skin side up, on a rack in the sink. Boil a kettleful of water and immediately pour the water evenly over the skin, allowing it to drain straight away. The skin will mostly dry quickly as the residual hot water evaporates, but blot it with kitchen paper or a clean cloth to make absolutely sure. Then salt and roast as normal.

If the meat is cooked and the diners assembling, but the crackling has failed to crisp up, free it – as a sheet – from the meat and leave the latter to rest. Put the crackling in a roasting tin and return it to a moderately hot oven, 200°C, 400°F, Gas mark 6, for 5–10 minutes. Cut it into strips using scissors.

Roast Loin of Pork with Sage & Onion Puddings

serves
6

a piece of pork loin, about 2.5kg
   (5½lb)
150ml (5fl oz) dry white wine
generous 1 tablespoon plain flour
250ml (9fl oz) stock
   (pork or chicken)
salt and pepper

For sage & onion puddings
pork or beef dripping for frying,
   and for the pudding tins
1 small onion, peeled and chopped
half the quantities given for Yorkshire
   Pudding (see page 25)
12 sage leaves, chopped

Preheat the oven to 230°C, 450°F, Gas mark 8. Prepare the pork for roasting in a tin. Calculate the roasting time. Roast for 20 minutes, then reduce the heat to 170°C, 325°F, Gas mark 3. After about 1 hour, add the white wine to the tin.

Meanwhile, prepare the sage and onion puddings. Melt the fat in a frying pan and cook the onion gently until translucent. Turn off the heat and allow to cool.

Cook the meat until done, checking from time to time. Remove from the oven and allowed to rest for at least 20 minutes before carving. Turn up the heat to 220°C, 425°F, Gas mark 7.

Make the Yorkshire pudding batter, then stir in the cooled onion and the chopped sage. Using a muffin tray or deep-holed bun tin, put 1 scant teaspoon of fat in each mould and then put into the oven to heat. When the fat is smoking hot, take the muffin tray out and add 1–2cm (½–¾in) to each mould. Return to the oven and cook for 15–20 minutes, or until puffed and golden, and done in the middle.

To make the gravy, pour all the juices out of the roasting tin into a bowl. Set aside for a few minutes then remove as much fat as possible to a separate container.

Put about 2 tablespoons of the fat back into the roasting tin and add the flour. Stir well over low heat, allowing the flour to brown. Stir in the defatted juices, scraping up any residue stuck to the tin. Gradually add the stock (you may not need it all), stirring well, and bring to the boil. Season to taste.

Pork with Garlic & Herb Paste

serves 4

a piece of belly pork, weighing about
  2kg (4½lb)
1 tablespoon each of fresh sage,
  rosemary and mint, finely chopped
8 garlic cloves, peeled and crushed
grated zest of 1 lemon (preferably
  unwaxed)
a good pinch of finely ground allspice

a good pinch of finely ground
  coriander
1–2 tablespoons olive oil
a splash of white wine or stock
about 1 tablespoon plain flour
1 teaspoon salt
a generous grind of black pepper

Put the pork on a board and carefully cut through the fat layer between the skin and the meat (it helps if the pork is well chilled). Aim to leave just under 1cm (½in) fat attached to the skin, but don't worry too much if it is not possible. Keep the skin on one side and put the meat, bones down, in a roasting tin.

Mix all the ingredients except the white wine and flour to make a paste. Spread this evenly over the top of the meat. Put the skin back on top. Leave to marinate for 2–3 hours.

Preheat the oven to 140°C, 275°F, Gas mark 1 and put the pork in to cook. Allow at least 60 minutes per 500g, possibly a little longer. It will yield a lot of fat and some deep-brown juices.

When the meat is cooked, remove it to a warmed plate. If the crackling hasn't crisped, put it in a shallow tin, turn the oven up to 200°C, 400°F, Gas mark 6 and return it to cook for 10–15 minutes, checking progress occasionally. Pour off all the fat and juices from the roasting tin into a bowl. Deglaze the tin with white wine or stock and add to the juices. Skim off the fat.

Put 2 tablespoons of fat back into the roasting tin and add a little flour, stirring with a wooden spoon over a low heat. Allow the flour to cook and brown a little, then stir in the cooking juices, and a little more stock if necessary, to produce gravy.

To serve, cut the meat in slices. This is best served with cabbage and plainly cooked potatoes – mashed, or small whole new ones.

Slow-Roast Belly Pork with Root Vegetables & Oriental Flavourings

serves
4

a piece of belly pork, weighing about
　　1.5kg (3½lb), with the skin scored
2–3 large baking potatoes
1 large carrot
1 sweet potato
2 large parsnips
2–3 small white turnips, or about
　　one-third of a larger yellow turnip
about 1 tablespoon oil or pork dripping
fresh root ginger, about 2cm (¾in),
　　peeled and cut into long matchsticks
a few shallots, peeled and halved
　　lengthways

6–8 garlic cloves, peeled but left whole
salt

For the oriental flavourings
2–3 whole star anise
generous 1 teaspoon whole black
　　peppercorns, lightly crushed
40g (1½oz) honey
2 tablespoons soy sauce
2 tablespoons dry sherry
200–300ml (7–10fl oz) chicken stock
　　(keep about a third of this back for
　　the end)

Preheat the oven to 220°C, 425°F, Gas mark 7. Give the pork the boiling water treatment (see page 61), and salt lightly. Mix all the oriental flavourings in a small bowl. Wash, trim and peel all root vegetables. Cut into chunks. Put them in a pan, of cold water and boil for about 2 minutes. Drain thoroughly. Heat the oil in a roasting tin until very hot, add the vegetables and turn them. Mix in the ginger, shallots and garlic and pour into the tin, laying the pork on top, skin side up.

Roast for 15 minutes, then reduce the heat to 150°C, 300°F, Gas mark 2. Cook for 2–3 hours; stir the vegetables once or twice.

About 30 minutes before you want to eat, turn the heat back up to 200°C, 400°F, Gas mark 6. Stir the vegetables, then return the tin to the oven. When the crackling is crisp, remove the meat to a warmed serving platter. Arrange the vegetables around it. Keep hot.

Skim the fat off the juices left in the roasting tin. Taste and add more salt if needed. Use hot stock to thin and deglaze any residue in the tin, then pour all juices, into a gravy boat.

Loin of Pork Stuffed with Spinach

serves
4

1kg (2¼lb) boned pork loin
a little lemon zest (preferably
    unwaxed), finely grated
1 tablespoon olive oil
salt and pepper

For the spinach stuffing
250g (9oz) spinach, any thick stems
    removed
50g (2oz) parsley, stems removed
½ teaspoon salt
freshly ground black pepper

Buy a piece of pork loin with a good proportion of lean meat. Remove the skin
with the fat beneath, plus the 'tail' of fatty meat. Use a sharp knife to separate
the thin white covering of sinew from the lean neatly.

Place the meat so that the grain is at right angles to you. Take a sharp knife and
make a cut into the left side, parallel to the grain and about one-third of the way
down from the top. Don't cut all the way through – leave a 'hinge' at the right-
hand side. Now start at the right-hand side and repeat the action, cutting about
one-third of the way up from the bottom, leaving the 'hinge' at the left.

Open out the meat as a single sheet. Sandwich it between two pieces of
greaseproof paper and beat out with a rolling pin until it is roughly 1½–2 times
larger, and about half the original thickness. Season with the lemon zest, salt and
coarsely ground black pepper. Put to one side while you make the stuffing.

Wash the spinach and pack into a saucepan. Cook over high heat for a couple of
minutes, stirring until it has wilted. Add the parsley and cook just enough to
soften it. Remove from the heat, press into a sieve to get rid of the liquid. Put the
mixture on to a board and chop coarsely. Season with the salt and pepper.

Take the meat and spread the spinach and parsley mixture over it, leaving about
an inch all round. Roll up like a Swiss roll and tie firmly with string. Preheat the
oven to 200°C, 400°F, Gas mark 6. Put the olive oil in a small roasting tin, then
add the meat and roast for about 50 minutes. Check to make sure the outside isn't
cooking too fast, and season the outside with salt about halfway through cooking.
To carve, simply cut in thin slices.

Pork Marinated to Taste like Wild Boar

serves 6–8

2.5–3kg (5½–6½lb) leg of pork, boned and skinned
400ml (14fl oz) pork chicken or veal stock
3 tablespoons plain flour
salt and pepper

For the marinade
300ml (10fl oz) red wine
50ml (2fl oz) red wine vinegar
½ onion, peeled and sliced
2 shallots, peeled and sliced
2 garlic cloves, peeled and crushed
3 bay leaves, crushed
8–10 thyme sprigs
a few parsley stalks, roughly chopped
12 black peppercorns, bruised
12 juniper berries, bruised
3 cloves, bruised
zest of ½ orange (preferably unwaxed), cut in long strips
1 teaspoon salt

Put all the marinade ingredients in a saucepan and bring to the boil. Allow to cool. Lightly score the fat of the meat in a diamond pattern. Put it in a deep bowl, and pour the cooled marinade over the meat. Turn it in the mixture, then cover and store in the refrigerator, where it can marinate for up to 4 days. Turn the meat a couple of times each day.

When ready to cook, preheat the oven to 220°C, 425°F, Gas mark 7. Remove the meat from the marinade. Strain the latter, reserving the liquid. Put the meat on a rack in a roasting tin and add a little water to the base of the tin. Cook for 20 minutes, then reduce the heat to 170°C, 325°F, Gas mark 3 for a further 2 hours, or until done. Baste with the reserved marinade at intervals and check that the liquid in the tin doesn't burn. If it becomes too deep brown, add a little more water to the tin – the gravy is very rich but will burn easily.

When the meat is cooked, remove to a warm serving dish and allow it to rest. Pour all the fat and juices from the tin into a bowl, then deglaze the tin with a little of the stock and add this to the juices. The fat will rise to the surface – skim off as much as possible. Put about 3 tablespoons of the fat back into the tin and sprinkle in the flour. Stir well and allow to cook gently over low heat. Once it has turned a creamy colour, gradually stir in the reserved cooking juices, then the stock. Taste and check the seasoning before serving.

Roast Ham with Rhenish Wine

'Rhenish' wine (from the Rhineland vineyards) was much appreciated in Britain during the 17th and 18th centuries. Whether it had the same perfumed notes and degree of sweetness that it does today is not clear, but this recipe, after one given by John Thacker in 1758, is worth trying.

serves
6–8

a piece of unsmoked ham weighing
    about 2–2.5kg (4½–5½lb)
a handful of cloves (optional)
1 bottle light, medium-sweet German
    wine, such as Niersteiner

scant 2 tablespoons plain flour
200ml (7fl oz) light stock
salt and pepper

Follow the supplier's instructions about whether or not to soak the ham.

When ready to cook, carefully remove the skin from the ham (try to leave most of the fat in place). If desired, score the fat and stud with cloves. Place the meat on a rack in a roasting tin and pour the wine in underneath.

Preheat the oven to 220°C, 425°F, Gas mark 7. Roast the meat for 30 minutes, then reduce the heat to 170°C, 325°F, Gas mark 3. Continue to cook, basting at frequent intervals with the wine. If this shows signs of drying up and catching, add a little water.

When the ham is done, remove to a warm serving plate to rest. Pour all the roasting juices into a bowl, allow the fat to rise and skim off as much as possible. Put about 2 tablespoons of the fat back in to the roasting tin and sprinkle in a little flour. Stir well, and allow to cook gently for a few minutes. Then gradually stir in the juices, scraping well with a wooden spoon to incorporate any residue from the base and sides of the roasting tin. Bring to the boil and stir in some stock to make a lightly thickened gravy. Check for seasoning: it is unlikely that much, if any, salt will be needed, but some pepper is a good addition. Also, if the meat has been cooked plainly, a couple of cloves crushed to powder can be added at this stage, to give just a hint of spice.

Serve with roast or mashed potatoes and greens.

Roast Ham or Gammon

When cooking ham, boiling is often thought of as the standard method, but opinions have always been split over this, and both spit-roasting and baking were also used. There are two basic ways to finish a ham, either by glazing or by dredging with breadcrumbs, recalling 17th- and 18th-century spit-roasts.

<table>
<tr><td>serves
8</td><td>a piece of uncooked ham or gammon,
    without skin, weighing 2kg (4½lb)
a handful of cloves (optional)
a glaze or breadcrumb coating
    (see below and page 81)</td></tr>
</table>

Follow the supplier's instructions about whether or not to soak the ham. If the piece of meat is to be served glazed, score the fat in diamonds at about 2cm (¾in) intervals and stud with cloves.

Preheat the oven to 170°C, 325°F, Gas mark 3, then put the meat in a roasting tin and cover with foil. Bake for 30 minutes per 500g, and 30 minutes extra. For the last 30 minutes, remove the foil to allow the outside of the joint to brown, or use one of the finishes over the page.

Glaze for Ham

125ml (4fl oz) whisky, preferably
without smoky character
125g (4½oz) demerara sugar

zest of ½ orange (preferably unwaxed),
cut in very thin strips
1 piece of star anise (optional)

Mix together all the ingredients, without dissolving the sugar. About 30 minutes before the end of cooking time, remove any covering from the meat and pour this mixture over it. If some of the sugar crystals remain on top, so much the better, because they will crisp a little during cooking. Use the mixture that runs into the tin and combines with the cooking juices to baste the meat at frequent intervals during the remaining cooking time.

Breadcrumb Coating for Ham

4 tablespoons breadcrumbs made from
stale white bread
1 tablespoon very finely chopped parsley

The breadcrumbs are best made by putting a couple of slices of stale white bread in a low oven. Leave them until they are dried out and pale gold, then remove, cool and crush. The crumbs need to be quite fine: pulverise the bread in a food processor or beat it in a mortar to reduce it as much as possible. Then rub through a wire sieve. Most will pass through to become near-powder. A few will remain in the sieve, but the process should reduce these to a degree of fineness that is acceptable, so use these too and mix in the parsley.

Put the mixture on a sheet of greaseproof paper. About 30 minutes before the end of cooking time, remove the foil from the meat and roll the side with the fat on over the crumb mixture, using the paper to help pat it over the surface. Return to the oven and cook for a further 30 minutes or until the coating is golden brown.

Leftovers

BRITISH COOKERY TRADITIONS aren't strong on recipes for cold pork. The reasons are not obvious – perhaps it is to do with fresh pork being less ubiquitous than beef and mutton. Or perhaps it is simply that pork is pleasant to eat cold with salad and bread and needs little help. Certainly, pork is good with pickles and chutneys of the old-fashioned type, especially mustardy ones like piccalilli, which cut the fat. Ham is another matter: it is more often eaten cold than hot. Ham salad has been a popular choice for a Sunday or other celebratory tea for 200 years, and the meat has probably been filling sandwiches for as long.

'Fresh' Pea & Ham Soup

Stock from ham bones is traditionally used to make soup with dried peas – i.e., peas that have been stored for winter. There is nothing wrong with this and it can be very good; but we now tend to think of frozen rather than dried peas and these, too, make good soup – if a little different from the standard article.

serves
4

1 litre (1¾ pints) well-flavoured
    ham stock
500g (1lb 2oz) frozen garden peas
a little cooked ham, cut in dice
    (optional)

salt and pepper
chopped fresh parsley or coriander,
    to garnish

Put the stock on to heat and add the peas. Bring to the boil and cook gently for about 10 minutes, then blend to a purée (this will have a slightly rough texture).

Return to the pan and reheat, seasoning with salt and pepper to taste. If you have any leftover ham, cut it in small dice and add these too. Serve with a little chopped parsley or coriander in each bowl.

Mustard Butter for Ham Sandwiches

The British – or at least, the English – have been making ham sandwiches for about 200 years, possibly longer. Mustard, usually of the pungent, bright yellow variety, was regarded as indispensable for these, at least for most of the 20th century. This is fine, but sometimes I prefer the Germanic tradition of mild, sweet mustard. Hence this flavoured butter.

makes 4–6

60g (2½oz) unsalted butter, softened
20g (¾oz) mild Dijon mustard
20g (¾oz) soft light brown sugar
1 dessertspoon lemon juice

Mix all the ingredients together thoroughly. Taste, and add more mustard, sugar or lemon juice if desired. Spread on slices of good sourdough bread, and top with layers of ham, cut as thinly as possible.

Hashed Meat

serves 4

about 500g (1lb 2oz) cold roast pork
    or other meat, thinly sliced

For the marinade

2 tablespoons leftover gravy or
    concentrated stock
1 tablespoon red wine vinegar
1 tablespoon redcurrant jelly
½ teaspoon salt
½ teaspoon ground black pepper
a little pounded mace
rosemary and a little sage
1 small onion, peeled and sliced
    in thin rings
a few celery leaves, chopped (optional)
1 tablespoon chopped parsley
1 tablespoon red wine or Marsala

For the broth

125g (4½oz) onion, peeled
30g (1oz) celery
60g (2½oz) carrots
60g (2½oz) turnips
a small bunch of parsley
60g (2½oz) good dripping
600ml (1 pint) stock or
    water, heated
the trimmings and any bones
    from the roast

For the sauce

30g (1oz) unsalted butter
30g (1oz) plain flour
salt and pepper

For the marinade, put the gravy in a small pan with 4 tablespoons hot water, then add the remaining ingredients. Warm gently, and as soon as the jelly has melted, remove from the heat. Cool and pour over the meat. Leave for up to 24 hours.

For the broth, finely chop the vegetables and parsley. Melt the dripping and add all the vegetables. Fry briskly, stirring frequently until they begin to brown at the edges. Add the hot stock plus any roast trimming from the roast. Simmer for about 1 hour and strain into a bowl and allow to cool. Lift off the surface fat.

Shortly before serving the hash, make the sauce. Melt the butter and stir in the flour. Cook gently for a few minutes, then gradually stir in the broth and bring to a simmer, stirring to make a smooth sauce. Lift the meat out of the marinade. Strain the latter and add the liquid to the sauce, stirring well and returning to boiling. Turn the heat low and lay in the slices of meat. Allow it to heat thoroughly (don't let the mixture boil, as it will toughen the meat), then serve.

Pork Rissoles with South-East Asian Spicing

makes
18–20

150g (5oz) cold roast pork, trimmed of skin, gristle and overcooked outside bits

50g (2oz) unsmoked bacon, without rind

2 mild green chilli peppers (or to taste), de-seeded

1 garlic clove, peeled

1 lemongrass stalk, washed and trimmed of its outer layer

a small handful of green coriander sprigs, washed

2 spring onions, washed, trimmed and finely sliced

oil or fat, for shallow frying

1 egg

½ teaspoon salt

Cut the cold pork and the bacon into rough chunks, put into a food processor and process to a mixture with the texture of coarse breadcrumbs.

Roughly chop the chillies, garlic and lemongrass, and whizz them in a blender, together with the coriander, to a coarse paste. Stir into the meat, then add the spring onions, salt and egg, and mix to a paste.

Heat a little oil in a frying pan and drop in generous teaspoonfuls of the mixture to make flat little cakes. Fry briskly for a couple of minutes, then turn and fry until both sides are golden brown. Drain on kitchen paper.

If you prefer not to fry the rissoles, they can be dropped on to a lightly greased baking sheet and cooked in the oven for about 10 minutes at 180°C, 350°F, Gas mark 4. Turn once halfway through cooking. Serve the rissoles with salad.

Flavourings

The flavouring amounts are suggestions; alter them to taste. Chillies can be very variable in strength. Lemongrass can be a bit tired and stale – but if it lacks zing, be careful about adding too much, as it also has a woody, resistant texture, which can be unpleasant.

Rissoles with Parmesan Pastry

makes 18–24

250g (9oz) cold roast lean meat,
    trimmed of skin and gristle
leftover gravy (or use broth,
    see page 61)
salt and pepper

For the pastry
100g (4oz) plain flour, plus extra
    for dusting
1 large egg, separated
50g (2oz) unsalted butter, softened
50g (2oz) Parmesan, finely grated
1–2 tablespoons water
vegetable oil, for deep frying

To make the pastry, put the flour in a bowl or on a slab, make a hollow and drop the egg yolk in. Add the butter and Parmesan and work together with your fingertips until it begins to form a paste. Add a little water and work together for a couple of minutes to make a smooth, soft dough. Cover and leave to rest while you prepare the filling.

Mince the cold meat finely; use a knife so that a little texture is retained. Mix with a few tablespoons of gravy to give a mixture that is moist but not runny. Add seasoning to taste – a little salt and pepper plus anything else that seems appropriate.

Dust a work surface with flour and roll the pastry out thinly (take care that it doesn't stick). For best results, it should be about the thickness of a twopence piece. Cut out circles with a diameter of 7cm (2¾in). Heap 1 generous teaspoon of filling on one side of each circle. Brush the edge of the pastry with a little egg white, then fold each circle of pastry in half to enclose the filling. Press the edges together gently to make shapes like tiny Cornish pasties, and give them a few minutes to firm up. Pastry trimmings can be pressed together and re-rolled to make more rissoles.

Heat the oil in a deep-fat fryer to 180°C, 350°F, Gas mark 4 and fry the rissoles until the pastry is golden brown. Remove with a slotted spoon, drain on kitchen paper, and serve immediately. If you prefer, the rissoles can be baked for 10 minutes at 180°C, 350°F, Gas mark 4.

Potted Ham

A good method for using up cold ham. Potting started off with raw meat cooked specifically for the purpose (it was actually a means of preserving, on a similar principle to French *confit d'oie*). Over the years, the recipes changed and became lighter and softer (and eventually evolved into the various 'pastes' sold as sandwich fillings).

serves
4

250g (9oz) cold cooked ham
freshly ground black pepper
ground mace, allspice or star anise
125g (4½oz) unsalted butter, softened

Take a piece of cold ham and remove any gristly bits, skin and connective tissue, and any outside edges that have hardened and browned in cooking (these can all go in the stockpot). Fat (unless there is an excessive amount, which is unlikely these days) can be incorporated into the potting process. Cut the ham into small chunks and then blitz it in a food processor. Add some black pepper and your other chosen seasonings. Mace and allspice are traditional; star anise isn't, but a suspicion, finely pounded, is good. Don't overdo the seasoning, and if you choose to add star anise, don't mix it with any other spices but pepper, and add a very small pinch – otherwise, it will be overpowering.

Beat the softened butter until creamy and mix in the seasoned ham. Put the mixture into a serving dish, such as a china soufflé dish, then chill. Serve for lunch or tea, with hot toast or good bread.

Chicken, Guinea Fowl & Quail

TOGETHER WITH DUCKS and geese, these birds are classified as poultry – domestic birds reared for the table. With the exception of quail (which were always wild birds until the development of quail farming in the second half of the 20th century), these were small, adaptable, farmyard scavengers. They were often seasonal, and were sought after as delicacies at particular times of the year, but as domestic birds they had less status than game, and were more accessible to the general population. Chickens, especially, could be kept in very small spaces.

We buy chickens all year round, expecting them to be tender and varying in price according to weight, along with other factors relating to the way in which they are produced. Our ancestors priced chickens differently – by age and time of year. In 1845, Eliza Acton wrote:

Fowls are always in season when they can be procured sufficiently young to be tender. About February they become dear and scarce; and small spring chickens are generally very expensive. As summer advances they decline in price.

This relates directly back to the cycle of egg-laying and hatching, which was at its lowest point in mid-winter, but increased dramatically as soon as the days began to lengthen. The majority of birds hatched around Easter flooded the market and the price came down as summer went on. They grew much more slowly than modern commercial stock – whose swift growth rate would have seemed extraordinary to farmers in the past.

A spring chicken really was a spring chicken – hatched in mid- to late winter, and ready for the table as a luxury in spring. It was simply roasted and appreciated for its tender flesh and delicate flavour. Smaller birds, the equivalent of poussins, were available, and were often grilled; older fowls were also plentiful, but were more suitable for boiling. Capons (castrated cockerels) were also once much esteemed, as they grew to be large, fat table birds.

Generally, we favoured young tender chickens – and that is what we now get, but at the price of compromising production systems, with repercussions for the welfare of the live birds, and a loss of flavour. It is difficult now to imagine what a luxury a roast chicken was right up until the 1960s.

Domestic chickens have come a very long way from their probable origin as wild south-east Asian jungle fowl that were slowly domesticated and gradually spread westwards, arriving in the British Isles shortly before the Roman conquest. From then, they scratched around farmyards, dunghills and urban backyards, probably with little change over the centuries – until, like all other farm animals, they began to receive the attention of agricultural improvers in the 18th and 19th centuries. They were improved by an input from Asian strains, which caused quite a stir because of their often very decorative appearance. The process by which the changes happened is largely unrecorded, because poultry breeding was generally a hobby for the urban working class, especially in the north of England. That said, many ladies – including Queen Victoria herself – kept fancy poultry as ornamental birds.

The counties around London, especially Surrey, Kent and Sussex, specialised in producing fat chickens for the London market, which showed a preference for white-fleshed birds. In the late 19th century, the creatures were crammed with oatmeal to give a fine flavour and texture. The ideal table fowl was required to have lots of tender white breast meat and light bones; economics, as always, looked for a bird that was early maturing. 'Sussex' breeds of hen developed from this demand, and the characteristics can still be detected in birds reared for the broiler system developed in the 1950s. The commercial breed used currently is the Ross Cobb, bred to gain weight as fast as possible and provide large amounts of white meat. In free-range systems with good feed, it can produce a fine chicken, but doesn't show its best side when subjected to intensive broiler production.

At tables in the past, a plain roast chicken with bread sauce and some type of stuffing was considered fine material for a Sunday dinner, and in the 18th century was served as a delicacy as part of a larger meal of multiple dishes. The traditional accompaniment of bread sauce dates back to the Middle Ages, when breadcrumbs were used to thicken and bind spiced sauces, although it was often badly made, with a texture described by Colonel Kenney-Herbert as being 'like a bread poultice'. The use of other flavours and sauces with chicken followed the general trends over the centuries, but the British seem to have developed dishes using large amounts of pungent aromatics such as tarragon or garlic under French influence.

Chicken has many other advantages. Roast chicken is excellent cold, and was a good dish for a ball supper (especially with mayonnaise and salad), or for a picnic (an event much enjoyed by the English, despite the weather, and one that was a feature of 19th-century social life). The meat could be made into many other dishes, and the bones produce good stock – so they were always sought after. Somehow, despite the current unease about intensive systems for rearing chickens, the meat has never quite lost its image as a treat.

Guinea Fowl and Quail

Neither of these birds is related in any way to chickens, but both are farmed for their meat in Britain. They have white flesh and flavours that are in the same range as chicken. Sometimes they are classed with game – guinea fowl because it is gamier than chicken and shares the same tendencies as pheasant to dryness, and quail because in the past it was available only as a wild bird.

Guinea fowl are indigenous to Africa; known in parts of the Mediterranean by Classical times, they became more widespread in early modern times through links between Guinea and Portugal (hence the English name). The live birds have attractive spotted plumage and a rounded, bustling shape. They have been used in British cookery since the 16th century or before, but there are few specific recipes for them, and they were often treated like turkey.

As wild birds, European quail are often summer visitors to south-eastern Britain, but seem to be unobtainable unless you go out and shoot them yourself. The farmed birds are a domesticated variety, Japanese quail, which are usually very small and delicately flavoured. They are often treated in a similar manner to other small game birds in the English kitchen.

Buying, Storage and Preparation

As a child, I was privileged to live on a farm with ample opportunity to observe some (very) free-range hens. My favourite source now is a local farm shop run by a woman who takes enormous pride in her poultry flock, and an equal pride in their presentation – plump, properly plucked, nicely trussed, complete with giblets. The flavour is excellent. If buying in a supermarket, look at the quality symbols and aim for one that ensures the optimum in terms of space, access to outdoors. The ability to range freely and a diet rich in grain both make a difference to the flavour.

Quality labels can help in making a choice. French Label Rouge birds should have been reared under excellent conditions with the best flavour in mind. They will be expensive. Supermarkets often have their own premium ranges, which make claims about welfare and feed. Individual producers (who mostly sell via their own shops and networks, or over the internet) often give a lot of detail about the conditions under which their birds are reared. Transparency in labelling, and in both supplier and producer, are all-important with chicken and poultry in general. The more anonymous a product, the less likely it is to have been treated with care at any stage.

Guinea fowl and quail also suffer from intensive rearing. It is difficult to know exactly what system has been used; generally you should assume this will have been intensive, unless stated otherwise. Both these birds are often imported, from unknown welfare systems abroad.

When buying chicken, a poussin is a very small young bird, weighing 450–500g (1lb–1lb 2oz), which will feed one person. A chicken – an older bird, though perhaps no more than 6–8 weeks old – will weigh around 1.5kg (3½lb) and feed 4 people. Older, larger birds – up to about 2.5kg (5½lb), and sometimes bigger – will feed up to 6 people. Guinea-fowl meat is similar to that of a good free-range chicken but is leaner and gamier in flavour. The birds are also smaller than chickens, and generally weigh 1–1.5kg (2¼lb–3½lb). One bird will serve 3–4 people. For quail, allow 1–2 birds per person.

The less a chicken costs, the more likely it is to need attention when it arrives in the kitchen. Remove and discard all wrappings and any elastic bands used to truss the bird (if it is trussed with string stitched through from side to side, the chances are that it has been properly prepared, and you won't need to do much). Pluck out any stubs and bits of feather. Dry the skin with kitchen paper, and dry the inside of the bird as well. Remove any obvious bits of pipe and trim the skin of the neck neatly.

Chickens, and most other birds, used to arrive with a little package of giblets – the neck, heart, gizzard and liver. Use these, if there are any, to make stock (see below). Very few chickens seem to come with giblets now. From the cook's point of view, this is not a good development.

The purpose of trussing a chicken is to make it look neat, compact and well shaped; to keep it tidy without any projecting bits to scorch (especially important for spit-roasting), ultimately giving a plump-looking bird which would present well at table. In practice, when roasting birds in the oven, I find that a trussed one tends to be undercooked between the thigh and the body when the rest of the bird is done. For this reason, I tend to remove ties about two-thirds of the way through cooking.

Chicken Giblet Stock

Should you manage to acquire a chicken with giblets, check the liver carefully to make sure the dark green gall bladder has been discarded. Add the liver to a stuffing mixture, pâté or a ragù for pasta.

Put the remaining giblets in a small pan with a bay leaf, a few parsley stalks and a few pieces of onion, carrot and celery if available, cover with water and bring to the boil. Skim, then cover and leave to simmer gently for about an hour. Top up with more water if necessary. Strain, discarding the debris and reserve the stock for gravy.

Roasting Times

Chicken must always be well cooked. Underdone, it is a notorious source of food poisoning. Because of this, it is also better not to stuff the body cavity of the bird, as the heat may not reach the centre of the stuffing by the time the meat is done. Cook the stuffing in a separate dish. Occasionally a thin layer of stuffing or flavouring is spread between the skin and the meat of the breast , a method that adds flavour and fat to the meat underneath.

Chicken, like turkey, is sometimes served with little sausages and bacon as well as bread sauce, or barded with bacon like game birds. If you don't bard it, protect the breast with buttered paper or tinfoil during the early stages of cooking.

Standard instructions for roasting a chicken are to start it off at 200°C, 400°F, Gas mark 6 for 20 minutes, then reduce the heat to 180°C, 350°F, Gas mark 4 and cook for 20–25 minutes per 500g until the juices run clear. Examine the meat between the leg and the body; if any hint of pink shows here, or in the juices that flow from the thickest part of the thigh when pierced with a skewer, the bird needs further cooking. Starting the bird on its side, then turning on to the other side, and finally on to its back, during cooking helps it to cook evenly. Allow for resting after cooking time.

Basic Roast Chicken

serves
4–5

½ lemon
1 chicken, weighing 2kg (4½lb)
a few sprigs of fresh herbs, such as
    parsley, thyme or marjoram
    (optional)
2 unsmoked bacon rashers (optional)
unsalted butter

3–4 tablespoons white wine or water
stock from the giblets (see page 95)
    or other chicken stock
scant 1 tablespoon plain flour
freshly ground black pepper
½ teaspoon salt

Preheat the oven to 200°C, 400°F, Gas mark 6. Put the lemon (which could be one you've squeezed all the juice out of) into the body cavity of the bird, along with the herbs. Bard the breast with bacon if you wish, or spread a little butter on it. Also spread a little butter over the roasting tin (just enough to stop the bird sticking as it starts to cook), and put the bird in. Calculate the roasting time.

It's often better to start roasting a chicken on its side, especially if it is a large bird and your oven is an unreliable gas one like mine. Cover with a lid if the tin has one, or with a piece of oiled or buttered foil. Roast for about 20 minutes, then reduce the heat to 180°C, 350°F, Gas mark 4. After another 10 minutes, turn the bird on to the other side; cover and roast for another 15–20 minutes, then turn it on to its back. Add the white wine or water, cover, and return to the oven for another 30 minutes.

Remove the foil, then baste the bird well with the cooking juices and sprinkle the salt over the skin. Return, uncovered, to the oven for the remainder of the roasting time. Check every 10 minutes or so to make sure the juices aren't burning (a good chestnut brown is OK; black definitely isn't). If they show signs of overcooking, add a little water. The skin should crisp and brown nicely. Baste once or twice more with the cooking juices – this helps to produce a really crisp, tasty skin.

The bird is done when the juices from the thickest part of the leg run clear (pierce it with a clean skewer or the tip of a sharp knife). Make sure the meat around the hip joint between the leg and the body is fully done; there should be no trace of pink. If there is, return the bird to the oven for a few minutes.

When it is fully cooked, remove it from the roasting tin to a warm serving plate while you make the gravy. Pour all the juices into a bowl, deglaze the tin with a little stock and add the result to the rest of the juices. Return the tin to the heat, then add a couple of tablespoons of the fat that will have risen to the top of the cooking juices and stir in the flour, allowing it to cook gently and turn a nutty brown. Remove as much fat as possible from the remaining juice and then stir gradually into the mixture in the roasting tin. Stir in the giblet stock, taste and adjust the seasoning.

Roast Chicken with Orange & Lemon

Citrus fruits were favourite flavourings for all sorts of meat dishes by the late 16th century, when they were used in combination with sweet spices and dried fruit. This recipe uses orange and lemon only, producing a very intense, slightly sharp-flavoured gravy.

serves
4–5

1 chicken, weighing 2kg (4½lb)
juice and pared zest of 1 lemon
(preferably unwaxed)
juice and pared zest of 1 orange
(preferably unwaxed)

a few sprigs of fresh herbs, such as
parsley, thyme or
marjoram (optional)
splash of stock, to deglaze
salt and pepper

Start the chicken off as in the basic method (see page 96). When you turn the chicken on to its back, pour the fruit juices over. Cover again and return to the oven. About 30 minutes before the end of cooking time, uncover, baste, then salt the skin and add the zest, cut in thin strips, to the juices and return to the oven. Baste again a couple more times. Take special care to watch that the juices in the tin don't burn; add extra stock or water if necessary.

At the end of cooking time, the bird should have a deep gold-brown and very crisp skin. (Turn the oven up to 220°C, 425°F, Gas mark 7 for a few minutes to get it really brown and crisp at the end, if necessary, but do watch for burning.) There should be a relatively small amount of juice with a very concentrated flavour in the roasting tin. Pour off the juices and deglaze the tin with a little stock. Skim the fat off the juices and add the deglazed cooking residue, but don't attempt to make a thickened gravy – just give everyone a spoonful or two of the cooking juices with the meat.

Roast Chicken with Tarragon

The fresh, grassy, slightly aniseed note of tarragon is a classic partner for chicken in French cookery, with many variations on the theme, using poached or roast chicken, served hot or cold. Although recipes for the dish have appeared in several English cookery books over the last 100 years or so, it never seems to have become really popular, perhaps because French tarragon is not especially easy to grow in Britain (Russian tarragon, much more vigorous, lacks the flavour of the French variety). This is based on a recipe given by Elizabeth David in *Summer Cooking* (1965).

serves 4–5

a small bunch of fresh tarragon
60g (2½oz) unsalted butter
1 chicken, weighing 2kg (4½lb)
1 teaspoon grated lemon zest
   (preferably unwaxed), plus
   ½ the lemon

100ml (3½fl oz) white wine or
   chicken stock
generous 1 teaspoon plain flour
150ml (5fl oz) single cream
salt and pepper

Pick the leaves off the tarragon and chop them. Mix a generous tablespoonful of chopped leaves with most of the butter – leave about 15g (½oz) for finishing the sauce. Put the tarragon butter, and the ½ lemon, inside the bird. Roast as in the basic method given on page 96, basting from time to time with the cooking juices, turning it on to its back after 45 minutes, and seasoning with salt and pepper towards the end of cooking.

When the bird is cooked, remove it to a warmed plate and pour all the juices into a bowl. Deglaze the tin with the white wine, making sure it bubbles fiercely, or with a little chicken stock. Add all the herby, buttery juices back into the roasting tin. Add the lemon zest and the remaining butter worked together with the flour. Stir well, then add the cream and the rest of the chopped tarragon and heat until the sauce boils and thickens.

Roast Pullet with Gammon

The original for this recipe came from John Nott in *The Cook's and Confectioner's Dictionary* (1726). His recipes reflect the rich, meaty dishes popular among the aristocracy of the early 18th century. A pullet – a young laying hen – was an especially prodigal use of resources.

serves
4

100g (4oz) lean gammon (or unsmoked bacon, fat removed)
2 tablespoons finely chopped fresh herbs – a mixture of parsley, chives and basil

1 chicken, on the small side – about 1.5kg (3½lb)
olive oil or unsalted butter
splash of chicken stock, to deglaze
salt and pepper

Preheat the oven to 180°C, 350°F, Gas mark 4. Mince the gammon. In an 18th-century kitchen, some unfortunate maid or scullion would have had to do this on a board with two knives; for us, a food processor works very well. Mix the minced meat with the chopped herbs, then season; go easy on the salt, as the gammon will already be salty, but be fairly generous with the pepper.

Carefully ease the skin away from the flesh over the breast of the chicken. Divide the gammon and herb mixture in two and spread it over each side of the bird, between the meat of the breast and the skin. Pull the skin back and sew or skewer it at the neck so that the stuffing remains in place during cooking.

Spread a little olive oil or butter in a roasting tin and put the bird in. Cover the breast with a piece of tinfoil, as the skin cooks through quickly in this recipe. (Start the bird off breast down if this works better in your oven, but when you turn it on to its back, use a piece of tinfoil to protect the breast until cooking is nearly completed.) Calculate the cooking time (see page 87) and roast until the bird is three-quarters cooked. Then remove the foil, baste well, sprinkle the bird with salt and continue roasting until fully cooked.

Put the bird on a warmed platter to rest, removing any strings or skewers. Skim the fat off the cooking juices and deglaze with a little stock. Check the seasoning and serve.

Roast Guinea Fowl

Recipes for roasting guinea fowl – or guinea-hens, as they were sometimes called – appear from the 19th century onwards; the English usually seem to have treated the birds simply, regarding them in the same light as pheasants. They can be tricky to cook well, as the meat on the breast tends to cook through and dry out before the legs are fully cooked. Starting the bird on its side for 15 minutes, then turning it on to the other side for another 15 minutes, before finally turning it on to its back overcomes this to some extent.

serves 3–4

unsalted butter
2–4 rashers fat bacon
   (unsmoked streaky is best)
1 guinea fowl, about 1kg (2¼lb)

100ml (3½fl oz) port (optional)
150ml (5fl oz) well-flavoured
   chicken stock
salt and pepper

Lightly butter a small roasting tin in which the guinea fowl will fit nicely. Wrap the bacon around the breast of the bird and tie on with string.

Preheat the oven to 200°C, 400°F, Gas mark 6. Roast the bird for 20 minutes at this temperature, then reduce the heat to 180°C, 350°F, Gas mark 4 and cook for a further 25 minutes. Then remove the bacon, season with a little salt and continue to roast until the juices run clear. Allow to rest for about 10 minutes before serving.

To make the gravy, pour off all the cooking juices into a bowl and skim off and discard the fat that rises to the surface. Deglaze the roasting dish with the port, if using, or the chicken stock. Add the cooking juices and boil hard to produce a fairly small amount of thin, well-flavoured gravy. Adjust the seasoning with salt and pepper as necessary.

To accompany a guinea fowl, serve Bread Sauce (page 126). A Wild Rice Pilaf is very good with this (page 98. A salad of watercress was favoured as an accompaniment by 19th-century cookery authors, but, writing in 1905, Colonel Kenney-Herbert suggested a salad of cos lettuce dressed with wine vinegar, oil, and a seasoning of 1 teaspoon each of chopped tarragon and chives.

Wild Rice Pilaf

serves
3–4

20g (¾oz) dried chanterelles
125–150g (4½–5oz) wild rice
20g (¾oz) unsalted butter
1 medium onion, peeled and
    finely chopped

150–200g (5–7oz) chestnut mushrooms,
    washed, trimmed and sliced
50g (2oz) almonds, blanched and cut
    into slivers
1–2 tablespoons parsley, finely chopped
salt and pepper

Rinse the dried chanterelles and put in a small bowl; cover with boiling water and leave to soak. Put the wild rice in a pan and cover generously with boiling water; simmer gently until cooked, about 45 minutes. Melt the butter in a large frying pan and cook the onion gently, stirring from time to time until the pieces begin to turn a pale gold. Add the chestnut mushrooms and continue to cook gently, stirring occasionally until all the liquid they exude has evaporated.

When the wild rice is cooked, drain and stir into the onion-mushroom mixture. Drain the chanterelles and add these too. Check the seasoning and adjust as necessary. Toast the almonds for 5–10 minutes. Stir these and the chopped parsley through the wild rice mixture just before serving.

Cashew Nut Sauce

serves
3–4

40g (1½oz) unsalted butter
¼ small onion, peeled and very
    finely chopped
75g (3oz) raw cashew nuts

roux made with 15g (½oz) plain flour
    and 15g (½oz) unsalted butter
150ml (5fl oz) chicken or game stock
salt and pepper

Melt the butter in a small frying pan, add the onion and the cashew nuts and fry gently until the nuts become pale gold in colour. Empty the mixture into a food processor and whizz to a paste.

Use a small pan to make the roux, and once it is smooth and has cooked for a few minutes, stir in the nut paste plus enough stock to make a sauce. Season to taste and serve.

Roast Quail with
Vine Leaves & Grapes

In the United Kingdom, quail are almost always farmed, and generally very small. They are best quite plainly cooked, and the standard instruction in English cookery books of previous centuries was always to wrap them in vine leaves. This is a nice conceit, if you can beg or steal some fresh leaves from someone, although I'm not convinced it makes a great difference to the flavour.

serves
4

8 quail
a handful of small white seedless
  grapes
8 large vine leaves, if available
8 rashers unsmoked fat bacon, thinly
  cut, or unsmoked pancetta

unsalted butter, melted
100ml (3½fl oz) white wine
salt and pepper

Preheat the oven to 200°C, 400°F, Gas mark 6.

Season each bird with salt and pepper and pop a couple of grapes inside. Fold each bird in a vine leaf, then wrap a piece of bacon around it and tie in place with string. Brush each one with a little melted butter. Arrange the quail in a shallow roasting tin and pour over the white wine. Roast for 20–25 minutes, basting a couple of times with the wine and buttery juices.

Serve the quail still wrapped in their vine-leaf parcels, with the cooking juices, skimmed of fat. Game Chips go well with quail, and a green salad tastes better with quail than cooked vegetables.

Leftovers

A GOOD ROAST chicken is delicious cold as well as hot. Accompaniments can be very simple – some good bread, a well-made salad and a bottle of chilled white wine make it into a meal. Some more elaborate cold chicken dishes became classics of the English kitchen. Two are given below and on the following page, one from the late 19th century and the other devised for the coronation of Queen Elizabeth II. Although the recipes quoted are for whole chickens, they can easily be scaled down to cope with the remains of a bird already partly carved for a previous meal.

Julienne Soup

serves
4

125g (4½oz) carrot
40g (1½oz) turnip
125g (4½oz) celery
200g (7oz) asparagus
125g (4½oz) onion, peeled
40g (1½oz) unsalted butter
about 1 teaspoon chopped
   fresh tarragon

1 litre (1¾ pints) well-flavoured
   chicken stock
1 small lettuce
½ teaspoon granulated sugar
salt, to taste
a little chopped fresh parsley
finely grated Parmesan, to serve

Cut the carrot, turnip, celery and asparagus stems into batons about 2cm (¾in) long and 5mm (¼in) square (the asparagus tips can be left whole and reserved until the end of cooking). Slice the onion into fine slivers.

Melt the butter in a large saucepan. Add the vegetables and the tarragon, cover tightly, and cook over low heat for 15–20 minutes, stirring from time to time. Then add the chicken stock and simmer for about 10 minutes. At the end of this time, add the asparagus tips and the lettuce, cut into thin strips. Cook for 5–10 minutes longer. Add the sugar, and salt as you feel necessary. Ladle into soup bowls and garnish with chopped parsley. Hand the Parmesan cheese separately.

Mayonnaise of Fowl

serves 4–6

1 cold roast chicken
3 tablespoons olive oil
1 tablespoon wine vinegar
lettuce (inner leaves from soft, flat
    lettuces, or use lamb's lettuce)
mayonnaise

salt and pepper
tarragon, chervil or parsley, to decorate

Joint the chicken, separating the drumsticks from the thighs. Cut off the wings and divide into joints. Cut the breast meat into neat pieces. Mix the oil vinegar, a little salt and pepper, and marinate the chicken for 1–2 hours.

Make a bed of lettuce on a serving dish. Drain the chicken from the vinaigrette and arrange on the lettuce. Use mayonnaise to mask the chicken and decorate with the herbs. Serve immediately.

Chicken Sandwiches

makes 3–4

100g (4oz) cooked chicken, free of
    skin, fat and gristle
100g (4oz) cooked tongue
4 tablespoons mayonnaise
celery salt, or table salt

a pinch of cayenne pepper
anchovy essence (optional)
6–8 lettuce leaves
tarragon vinegar
6–8 slices of good white bread

Put the chicken, tongue and mayonnaise in a food processor and blend. Season with the celery salt (remembering that the tongue may be quite salty), cayenne pepper and the anchovy essence, if using.

Dip the lettuce leaves in tarragon vinegar, and put one on a slice of bread; spread a layer of the meat mixture over, top with another leaf and a slice of bread.

Chicken Sandwiches with Ravigote Butter

Another idea from Colonel Kenney-Herbert's *Common-Sense Cookery* (1905), given in a short section on sandwiches. Ravigote butter is not something generally found in the modern kitchen, but it is delicious and useful for all sorts of sandwiches. The name is derived from the French verb ravigoter, to perk up. Burnet, a salad herb of long-established meadows, has pretty oval leaves with serrated edges. Its flavour is reminiscent of cucumbers. It is not usually seen on sale, but can easily be grown in a pot or a sunny corner. If it is unobtainable, either omit it, or replace it with parsley, which gives the classic French fines herbes combination. This recipe makes quite a large amount but it can be frozen, or used with other dishes – with plain roast chicken or eggs, for instance. The recipe works equally well with turkey or ham.

makes 12

for the ravigote butter
30g (1oz) fresh chervil
30g (1oz) fresh tarragon
30g (1oz) fresh chives
30g (1oz) fresh burnet (optional)
250g (9oz) unsalted butter, softened

Pick over the herbs and wash them, then scald by placing in a small bowl and pouring boiling water over them. Leave for 2 minutes. Drain on kitchen paper, then put them in a blender and chop as finely as possible. Add the butter gradually, to achieve a paste that is as smooth as possible.

For sandwiches, take equal quantities of chicken or turkey and ham cut in julienne strips (the Colonel suggests also using tongue or *foie gras* similarly cut). Sandwich them between day-old slices of bread, thinly cut and spread with ravigote butter.

Half the suggested amount of herbs and butter is about right for 12 slices of average-sized sandwich bread. Because the chicken is cut into small strips, it doesn't matter if the less glamorously shaped pickings off the carcass are used.

Coronation Chicken

Devised for the coronation of Queen Elizabeth II in 1953, this could be regarded as a variation on the theme of chicken mayonnaise. The industrial versions used as sandwich fillings in the 1990s did few favours for what is, when well made, a delicious dish, which most people love.

serves 4–6

2 tablespoons sunflower oil
1 small onion, peeled and very finely chopped
1 dessertspoon curry powder (mild Madras)
generous 1 tablespoon mango chutney, rubbed through a sieve
250g (9oz) mayonnaise, home-made or good-quality bottled

1 cold roast chicken, skinned, boned and divided into neat, roughly bite-sized chunks
flaked almonds, toasted until golden brown
salt and pepper
lettuce leaves, lightly dressed with oil and vinegar, to serve

Heat the oil and fry the onion very gently until translucent. Stir in the curry powder and continue to cook gently until it loses its raw smell. Remove from the heat and allow to cool.

Stir in the mango chutney and the mayonnaise to make a thick, lightly curried cold sauce. Taste and adjust the seasoning. Arrange the chicken pieces on top of the lettuce leaves and pour the curried mayonnaise over. Scatter the almonds on top.

Turkey

In Britain, it's difficult to think of turkey without thinking of Christmas. When these birds first arrived, shortly after European explorers discovered the Americas, they were an exotic curiosity. However, they fitted into a recognisable place in the eating habits of the time – as a large bird among the many already served at the tables of the rich at great feasts and important occasions. Christmas was undoubtedly one of these; the association between the two developed early, on but not exclusively until the late 19th century.

Prices for turkeys were cited in London markets by the 1550s, when they were also mentioned in conjunction with Christmas by Thomas Tusser. By the 17th century, turkeys had spread across England – partly because they were novelties, albeit difficult ones (they detest wet conditions). Rearing turkeys became a speciality of East Anglia, especially Norfolk, in the 17th and 18th centuries. The birds were turned loose on the stubble after harvest to fatten on any stray corn, and were then driven, on foot, to the Christmas markets of large towns and to London.

Like chickens, turkeys were seasonal to some extent. Turkey poults (young birds) were very expensive in early spring, but prices dropped as the summer wore on, and into the autumn. But even in the first half of the 19th century, demand was by far the strongest in mid-December. Eliza Acton remarked 'The great demand for turkeys in England towards Christmas, and the care which they require in being reared, causes them to be brought much less abundantly into the markets when young, than they are in foreign countries; in many of which they are very plentiful and very cheap.'

Roasting a turkey in the past was obviously regarded as almost as much of an undertaking as it is now. Suggested spit-roasting times are relatively short by our standards. However, cooks were always entreated to make sure that the bird was fully done, preferably by allowing it time to come to room temperature before roasting – a reflection of the fact that the birds were mostly cooked in winter, and that old-fashioned larders were chilly. Another point noted by cookery writers in the past was that the sinews in a turkey's legs should be pulled (large birds develop tough sinews to keep them upright), and that doing so could be difficult. Mrs Roundell suggested shutting the bird's legs in the crack of a door, with one person inside holding the bird, and the other outside, pulling on the legs. We may be squeamish about such things, but a cook in a good household would have to know how to carry out such procedures in order to serve a bird that was considered properly dressed.

Turkeys were trussed like chicken for roasting, the wings and legs tied close to the body, sometimes with the gizzard of the bird under one wing, and its liver under the other. This English mode exasperated the Frenchman Alexis Soyer, who in 1849 considered that treating the liver this way would spoil the look of the bird once roasted (because it would drip juices down the side as it cooked), but the 'liver-wing' was considered a delicacy until the mid-19th century.

Stuffings and forcemeats of various descriptions were almost always used with turkeys by the 18th century, mostly in the crop (at the front of the breast). A standard English type of stuffing with herbs and lemon was one option, but mixtures using cooked veal, pork sausagemeat or chestnuts were often given. Pork products of various kinds, including sausages, have been consistently used with turkeys over the centuries. Eliza Acton suggested that the body of the bird could be filled with chestnuts stewed with ham or bacon. For a more elaborate dish, the bird could be made into a galantine by boning it, filling with forcemeat and sewing it up again before cooking. Hannah Glasse, in 1747, gave an early recipe for this under the title 'To roast a turky the genteel way', using a highly seasoned forcemeat based on veal or chicken. More usually wrapped in a cloth and simmered in water, this is a good way of dealing with a small bird.

The idea of a turkey as a special feast remains, despite intensive production and the demise of stubble-fed fowl. Acquire a well-produced bird and cook it gently, and think about the feasts of fowl – wild and domestic – enjoyed in the houses of the Elizabethan nobility.

Buying, Storage and Preparation

Even a small turkey weighs 4–5kg (8½–11lb) and will feed 8 people easily; monster birds of 8–10kg (17½–22lb) are quite usual, and likely to leave even a large family with a substantial quantity of leftovers. Most commercial turkeys are white-feathered, largely because British consumers, over the years, have shown a dislike for the dark pits left on the skin after black feathers have been removed. If this does not bother you, and the idea of a bird with slightly more flavour and slightly less breast meat appeals, try to find a Norfolk Black from one of the few suppliers who still take an interest in this breed. The internet is your best method for tracking these down, unless you happen to know someone who moves in the poultry-fancying or turkey-breeding worlds. A well-flavoured alternative is a Kelly Bronze, bred by the family after which it is named to have a deeper flavour than standard commercial stock, and reared under specified conditions (again, the internet will point you towards a supplier).

Remove a turkey from the packaging in which it arrives. Put it on a large dish or in a tin, dry with kitchen paper if it seems wet, and also blot the inside, checking that there are no odds and ends that shouldn't be there. Pick over it for any stray feathers and stubs, cover loosely and store in the bottom of the refrigerator. Remove it and allow it to reach room temperature for 1–2 hours before roasting.

Prepare stuffing in advance if it needs to cool before using. Stuff the crop only (not the body), to avoid the risk of heat not penetrating fully to the centre and the potential for food poisoning. The skin on the neck of the bird will have been left long to make a flap that can be folded over the back and sewn down to keep the stuffing in; you might like to make sure this is neatly trimmed. For birds generally, the cook was sometimes instructed to remove the merrythought (wishbone) beforehand, on the grounds that it makes carving easier. Turkey is perhaps the one bird where this is worth the effort, unless your family tradition is to pull the bone and make a wish across the Christmas table. Under the skin, you will find a line between the flesh of the breast (translucent and slightly pink) and the fat (opaque and creamy), forming the apex of a triangle with the point where the wishbone joins the keel of the breastbone. Cut along these lines with a small sharp knife to free the two long sides of the bone and then work the knife carefully around the top and the points where it meets the wing bones, one at either side. Whether you remove the wishbone or not, add the chosen stuffing, moulding it to give the bird a nice plump breast, and pull the skin back, sewing it down with thin string to prevent the stuffing escaping. Add the weight of the stuffing to that of the bird when you calculate the cooking time.

Roasting and Carving

Large turkeys are heavy and difficult to handle when hot. Make sure you have a large enough roasting tin and – if buying very large birds – that the turkey is not too big for the oven. It is also important that turkeys are properly cooked.

The meat has a tendency to dryness, which long cooking exacerbates. Methods suggested for counteracting this include marinating, barding, basting, and slow, gentle cooking. Marinating overnight in flavoured brine can help retain moisture. Bard with fat bacon, a butter-soaked cloth, or simply smear softened butter over the breast of the bird (especially if you intend to cook it lying on its back all the time). Basting by pouring the cooking juices and fat back over the bird fairly frequently is a good idea. Also effective is to start cooking with it lying on its side and then turning it, before finally turning it on to its back to complete cooking. Temperatures and times recommended for turkey vary enormously, and depend partly on size. As a guideline, I use 170°C, 325°F, Gas mark 3 for 30 minutes per 500g, but be guided by personal experience, the quirks of individual ovens and instinct.

When the bird is fully cooked, leave it to rest, covered, in a warm place. To carve, take slices of breast from back to front. Carve any stuffing or forcemeat in the crop across in slices. Then take off the legs and the wings (with a narrow outer portion of breast attached), and divide like those of a chicken, carving slices off the thighs and drumsticks.

Turkey Giblet Stock

Heat a little olive oil in a fairly large saucepan and add around 100g (4oz) bacon. Allow it to fry gently until it loses its translucency. Chop a peeled shallot, a leek, a celery stick, a carrot, a turnip, a handful of mushroom stalks and some fresh parsley. Add to the pan and turn up the heat. Cook briskly, stirring frequently, until the pieces begin to brown. Add the giblets of the bird, pour in 400ml (14fl oz) chicken stock or water, then bring to the boil and simmer gently for about 1 hour. Strain, discarding the debris, and skim off any fat. This stock can be prepared in advance and kept chilled.

The Italian Way of Roasting a Turkey

serves
8

4.5kg (10lb) oven-ready turkey
about 30g (1oz) unsalted butter
2–3 rashers unsmoked bacon
1 large carrot, chopped
1 onion, peeled and chopped
1 small white turnip, chopped
2 celery sticks, chopped
3 garlic cloves, peeled and chopped
2 large fresh rosemary sprigs
4–5 cloves
500ml (18fl oz) Giblet Stock
    (see page 19)
1–2 tablespoons arrowroot
salt

For the stuffing
unsalted butter
about 100g (4oz) unsmoked
    bacon, rind removed, chopped
    in small pieces
about 100g (4oz) good-quality
    sausage meat
100g (4oz) chestnut purée
3 prunes, pitted and chopped
1 small hard pear, peeled
    and chopped
75ml (3fl oz) Marsala
salt and pepper

Melt the butter, add the bacon and sausage meat, and fry gently for a few minutes. Stir in the chestnut purée, prunes, pear and Marsala, and season with a little salt and plenty of pepper. Cool and use to stuff the crop.

To cook the turkey, use a stout roasting tin. Smear the butter over the base, and put the bacon and vegetables in. Add the garlic, rosemary and cloves. Put in the turkey on its back, and add stock to cover the base of the tin. Season. Cover the whole with a sheet of tinfoil, crimping it firmly. Put the tin on the hob on the lowest heat. Braise the bird, gently, for about 1½ hours. Check occasionally, adding more liquid if necessary.

Preheat the oven to 180–190°C, 350–375°F, Gas mark 4–5. Move the turkey, still in the covered container, into the oven, and cook for another 45–60 minutes. Remove the foil, baste well, salt the skin and finish roasting, uncovered, for another 45 minutes. Add a little liquid if the juices look dry. When cooked, allow to rest. Tip everything left in the tin through a sieve, catching the juices in a bowl. Press with a wooden spoon to extract any liquid. Put the juices in a pan. Add about 250ml (9fl oz) stock. Finish by slaking the arrowroot with a little cold water; stir this into the gravy and reheat until just boiling and lightly thickened.

Alderman in Chains

serves
8

1 oven-ready turkey, about 4.5–5kg
 (10–11lb)
75g (3oz) unsalted butter, softened
8 sausages in a string
splash of Giblet Stock (see page 119),
 to deglaze
1–2 tablespoons arrowroot

For the green herb stuffing
150g (5oz) stale breadcrumbs

1 dessertspoon finely chopped fresh
 thyme or marjoram leaves
1 tablespoon finely chopped parsley
grated zest of ½ lemon (preferably
 unwaxed)
75g (3oz) beef suet, or unsalted
 butter broken into small pieces
1–2 medium eggs, beaten
1 teaspoon salt
freshly ground black pepper

For the stuffing, mix all ingredients together, adding the eggs last, to give a soft mixture. Use this to stuff the crop of the turkey, then sew the skin closed over it.

Preheat the oven to 170°C, 325°F, Gas mark 3. Calculate the roasting time (see page 119). Spread the softened butter over the bird and season well. Place it on one side in the roasting tin. Cook for about 45 minutes, basting every 15 minutes. Turn it on to the other side and baste well, then cook for another 45 minutes. Turn it on to its back and baste again, then protect the breast with a piece of foil and continue to cook, basting regularly.

About 45 minutes before the end of cooking time, put the sausages into a baking tray (don't cut the links) and put them in the oven to cook. About 15 minutes before the end of cooking time, remove the foil and allow the skin to brown. When the bird is fully cooked, rest for 20 minutes. Check the sausages, keeping them in a string.

Skim off any fat from the cooking juices and add the stock. Bring to the boil, scraping the tin. Mix the arrowroot with a little cold water and add to the juices. Heat gently until the arrowroot has become translucent and thickened the gravy.

Present the bird with the string of cooked sausages draped over the breast of the bird or around its front – the 'chains' of the pouting alderman.

French Forcemeat

An alternative stuffing for turkey, for those who like a meaty, savoury flavour. It can also be used for veal, or for rabbit or hare. For veal, use more sweet herbs; for rabbit or hare, add 300ml (10fl oz) cream. The original of this delicious recipe was given by John Thacker in 1758. About a century later, Eliza Acton was quoting essentially the same recipe, although without the typically 18th-century addition of anchovies. I've left them in, as it seems to me to suit modern tastes. Thacker was not specific about the uses of his recipe, but suggested replacing the veal with beef suet for stuffing a turkey – which would render the mixture inedibly fatty to us. Better to stick with veal, or if that is unobtainable, use chicken. Cooked lean veal left over from a roast can be used.

serves 6-8

75g (3oz) unsalted butter
2–3 open mushrooms, chopped (optional)
the liver of the bird, chopped (optional)
150g (5oz) lean cooked veal or chicken, minced
1 large teaspoon chopped fresh parsley
½ teaspoon fresh thyme leaves
grated zest of ½ lemon (preferably unwaxed)

2 anchovies, chopped
a generous pinch of freshly grated nutmeg
a pinch of cayenne pepper
a pinch of ground mace
50g (2oz) stale white breadcrumbs
a little stock or gravy
30g (1oz) unsmoked bacon, chopped
1 medium egg yolk
salt

Heat 50g (2oz) of the butter in a small frying pan. Cook the mushrooms and liver for a few minutes, then add the veal or chicken, parsley, thyme, lemon zest and anchovies. Season fairly generously with nutmeg and add a pinch of cayenne, a little mace and the breadcrumbs. Allow to cool, then tip into a food processor and whizz to a paste, adding a little stock if the mixture seems dry. Mix in the remaining butter, bacon and the egg yolk.

Note that Thacker says, 'take care you don't season it too high'. The best way to find out if the seasoning is right is to fry a trial spoonful and taste it. Only then add extra salt if you consider it necessary, as the anchovies and bacon will have contributed some saltiness already.

Chestnut Forcemeat

Chestnut stuffings go back at least as far as the first half of the 19th century in English cookery. This one is based on a recipe given by Eliza Acton (in 1845) and is good for turkey and game.

serves 8

150g (5oz) chestnut purée
75g (3oz) unsmoked bacon, rind removed, cut into small pieces
50g (2oz) stale white breadcrumbs
grated zest of ½ lemon (preferably unwaxed)

a pinch of freshly grated nutmeg
a pinch of cayenne pepper
1 medium egg
a little stock or milk
1 teaspoon salt

Mix together all the ingredients except the stock to make a smooth paste. If it seems a little on the dry side, stir in some stock or milk to slacken the mixture a little.

This mixture can be used as stuffing or made into 8 little cakes, floured and then fried gently.

Almond Sauce

serves 6

30g (1oz) unsalted butter
100g (4oz) ground almonds
30g (1oz) plain flour
250–300ml (9–10fl oz) stock

a pinch of ground mace
2 tablespoons single cream (optional)
a little salt

Melt the butter in a heavy saucepan and stir the almonds in over low heat. Cook very gently, stirring all the time, until the almonds are browned and toasted. Stir in the flour, then add the stock and continue to cook and stir until the mixture comes to the boil. Season with a little mace (which really does enhance this recipe) and salt. Finish by adding cream if you have some available.

Leftovers

CHRISTMAS DINNER IS possibly the one time of the year when the average British household finds itself with vast amounts of leftovers sitting in the refrigerator and demanding ingenuity in the using up, before everyone gets completely bored with the taste of turkey in curries, fricassees, pies, sandwiches and soup.

Devilled Turkey

serves
2

about 250g (9oz) cooked turkey
2 teaspoons Dijon mustard
½ teaspoon English mustard
   (made up, not powder)
½ teaspoon salt

2 heaped dessertspoons mango
   chutney – any large pieces of fruit
   in the chutney chopped fine
cayenne pepper, to taste
freshly ground black pepper

Prepare the turkey, pulling it into long, narrow pieces. The skin can be left on, as it crisps nicely under the grill. Mix the mustards, salt and chutney, adding as much cayenne as you feel desirable (try ¼ teaspoon if unsure) and a generous grind of black pepper. Rub the paste into the turkey pieces and leave in a cool place for 1–2 hours.

To cook, put the pieces under a preheated moderate grill for a few minutes. Keep a close eye on them and turn a couple of times, until they are well heated through. Any skin should turn quite crisp, and the edges of the pieces may brown, but try not to let them char. Alternatively, put them in a single layer in an ovenproof dish and bake in a hot oven, 220°C, 425°F, Gas mark 7, for 7–10 minutes.

Serve hot with rice and more chutney, or scatter over a salad of mixed leaves.

White Devil

In *The Tenth Muse* (1992), a collection of recipes from people he encountered while a member of the diplomatic corps, Sir Henry Luke gives a recipe specifically intended for white meat from turkey or other fowls. The result is pleasingly creamy and mildly piquant, and the heat can be increased by adding more slivers of fresh green or red chilli.

serves
4

280ml (9½fl oz) single cream
2 tablespoons Worcestershire sauce
1 teaspoon English mustard, or to taste

250g (9oz) cooked turkey breast meat,
    cut in neat pieces
fresh green or red chillies (optional)
salt

Put the cream in a saucepan and mix in the Worcestershire sauce and mustard. Heat rapidly until it boils. Stir in the turkey meat and allow to cook, very gently, until it is thoroughly hot. If using fresh chilli, remove the strings and seeds and cut the flesh into fine slivers. Add to the pan, then taste and correct the seasoning. Serve with boiled rice and a salad.

Turkey Soup

serves
4

1 litre (1¾ pints) well-flavoured
    turkey stock
a few celery leaves, finely chopped
about 100g (4oz) ham, diced
1 fresh red chilli pepper, finely diced
2 teaspoons nam pla (Thai fish sauce)

100g (4oz) cooked rice
salt
chopped fresh coriander
lime zest, preferably unwaxed, cut in
    fine slivers (optional)

Put the turkey stock in a large pan and bring to the boil. Add the celery leaves, ham, chilli pepper and nam pla, and cook for a few minutes. Add the cooked rice just before serving and let it heat through (it can be added earlier, but it makes the stock lose some of its clarity). Taste and add more salt if necessary. Ladle into bowls and add a sprinkle of chopped coriander and a little lime zest to each serving.

Turkey Pie

Turkey, chicken or veal and ham combinations are all traditional in pies in English cookery. Add mushrooms, or make a particularly good (if expensive) version by adding some of the white truffle and porcini paste sold in jars in Italian delicatessens.

serves 4–6

40g (1½oz) unsalted butter
150g (5oz) button mushrooms, sliced
40g (1½oz) plain flour
350ml (12fl oz) well-flavoured turkey stock
shortcrust pastry made with 100g (4oz) unsalted butter and lard mixed, and 200g (7oz) plain flour

40g (1½oz) white truffle and porcini paste (optional)
200–250g (7–9oz) cooked turkey, cut in neat pieces
125g (4½oz) cooked ham or gammon, cut in dice
1 medium egg, beaten
salt and pepper

Melt the butter in a saucepan and cook the mushrooms until all the liquid they exude has evaporated, but don't allow them to brown. Stir in the flour to make a roux, then add the stock gradually, stirring to produce a sauce. Season to taste and allow to cool.

When ready to bake, preheat the oven to 200°C, 400°F, Gas mark 6, and put a metal baking sheet in to heat.

Roll two-thirds of the pastry fairly thin and use it to line a pie dish about 20cm (8in) in diameter.

If using the truffle paste, mix it with the turkey meat. Distribute this, and the ham, over the pastry. Spoon the sauce in on top. Roll out the remaining pastry and use to cover the pie, sealing and crimping the edges. Cut a hole in the top for the steam to escape and decorate the surface of the pie with leaves made from the pastry trimmings. Brush with beaten egg.

Put the pie on the preheated baking sheet and cook for 15–20 minutes to set and crisp the pastry. Then reduce the heat to 180°C, 350°F, Gas mark 4, and bake for a further 20–25 minutes. Serve hot or cold.

Salsa for Turkey

Sometimes a 'sauce piquant' was served with devilled food in the 19th century. Recipes for it are based on a reduction of shallots and vinegar in butter, made into a flour-thickened sauce, which was further livened up with pepper, chilli or chopped gherkins. To us, the flavour is a bit contrived, but the vinegar-onion reduction suggested a tomato salsa – which usually contains raw onions, not to everyone's taste.

 serves 2–4

1 small shallot, peeled and very finely chopped
4 tablespoons white wine vinegar
1–2 tablespoons olive oil
1 beef tomato, skin and seeds removed, finely diced

1 garlic clove, peeled and crushed
a little chopped fresh red chilli
a pinch of granulated sugar
salt

Put the shallot and vinegar in a small pan and boil rapidly until the vinegar has evaporated. Pour into a small bowl and stir in the oil and tomato. Add the garlic and the chilli to taste, plus a pinch of sugar and a little salt.

This can be served with Devilled Turkey (see page 125), or added to a Club Sandwich (see below).

Club sandwich

Use three slices of toast per sandwich; spread the bottom layer with a little mayonnaise, add salad leaves (flat lettuce or lamb's lettuce), and 2–3 rashers crisp bacon; add a second layer of toast, then spread with a little more mayonnaise, top with thinly sliced turkey breast and a layer of salsa, and top with a final layer of toast. Press down firmly and cut obliquely to make triangular sandwiches.

Curry

There are so many curry pastes and marinades available that it may seem a bit redundant to give a recipe, but here is a delicious one based on Colonel Kenney-Herbert's spicing for a mild, coconut-flavoured Ceylon curry (he was emphatic that only fish, shellfish, veal or chicken should be added, but most things that work for chicken work for turkey as well). It can be spiced up with more chilli if desired.

serves 4

250–300g (9–10oz) onions, peeled and very finely chopped
50g (2oz) unsalted butter
1 teaspoon ground turmeric
2 teaspoons ground coriander
1 teaspoon ground cinnamon
½ teaspoon ground cardamom seeds
½ teaspoon chilli powder

½ teaspoon freshly ground black pepper
½ teaspoon salt
1 tablespoon grated fresh root ginger
400ml (14fl oz) coconut milk
400g (14oz) cooked turkey, cut in bite-sized chunks

Put the onions and butter in a heatproof casserole and fry gently until the onions begin to turn gold. Add the spices and salt, and cook gently for about 5 minutes, then add the ginger. Stir in the coconut milk and bring to the boil to make a smooth sauce. Allow this to cook gently for a few minutes longer, then stir in the turkey and continue to simmer for about 15 minutes so that the sauce reduces a little. It shouldn't be too runny.

Serve with rice and salad.

Sauces, Sides
& Vegetables

Bread Sauce

A traditional accompaniment for poultry and game birds in English cookery. Recipes vary in the flavourings – nutmeg and mace appear in some, and onions are more usual than shallots. Be guided by personal taste and family tradition.

serves
4

300ml (10fl oz) full-cream milk
2 cloves
75g (3oz) shallots, peeled

75g (3oz) fine breadcrumbs made
from slightly stale white bread
3 tablespoons single cream
salt and pepper

Put the milk in the top half of a double boiler or a bowl over simmering water. Stick the cloves into the shallots and leave to infuse for about 1 hour. Strain, discarding the shallots. Return the flavoured milk to the pan or bowl and stir in the breadcrumbs. Place over hot water again for about 10–15 minutes, during which the sauce should thicken up (not too much – if necessary add a little hot milk). Taste and add a little salt and pepper. Stir in the cream and serve.

A Sauce for Cold Meat

The original of this was given as 'A sauce for Partridge, or Moor Game' in the pompously named *Culina Famulatrix Medicinæ* published by Ignotus (otherwise known as Dr A. Hunter) in 1807. It produces a surprisingly modern result, and is also delicious with roast meat.

serves
4

4 salted anchovies, well rinsed
2 fat garlic cloves, peeled
juice of ½ lemon (you may not
need all this)

180ml (6fl oz) olive oil
cold roast meat, cut in small,
neat pieces
freshly ground black pepper

Put the anchovies, garlic, half the lemon juice and the oil in a blender and whizz together. Taste, and add more lemon juice if you wish; you might also like to add some pepper, although it is unlikely that any salt will be needed.

Mix with the roast meat. Serve this on a bed of salad leaves or with lightly cooked French beans, or broccoli spears, or small new potatoes.

Red Onion 'Marmalade'

serves 4

30g (1oz) unsalted butter
1 red onion, peeled, cut in half and
    sliced thinly
1 tablespoon sweet sherry

2 tablespoons red wine vinegar
a piece of star anise
20g (¾oz) light soft brown sugar
salt and pepper

Melt the butter in a small heavy frying pan. Add the onion, cover and cook very gently for about 30 minutes, stirring occasionally. It should become soft and translucent, but not brown.

Add the sherry and let it bubble a moment, then add the wine vinegar and a piece of star anise and bring the mixture to the boil. Stir in the sugar, season with a little salt and pepper, and simmer gently, stirring frequently, for another 15–20 minutes, or until it has achieved the consistency of runny jam. Remove the star anise before serving. Serve freshly made as an accompaniment to roast duck.

Cucumber Sauce

serves 4

½ cucumber, peeled, the seeds
    removed and the flesh cut into
    5mm (¼in) dice
½ small onion, peeled and finely
    chopped
250ml (9fl oz) red wine vinegar

30g (1oz) unsalted butter
a little ham or lean unsmoked bacon,
    finely chopped (optional)
2 tablespoons plain flour
250ml (9fl oz) good meaty stock or gravy
salt and pepper

Put the cucumber, onion and vinegar in a small bowl and leave to soak for 1 hour. Drain, discarding the vinegar, and blot the vegetables dry on kitchen paper.

Melt the butter in a frying pan. Add the ham or bacon and allow to brown a little. Then add the onion and cucumber and cook briskly until they are starting to brown slightly. Stir in the flour, then gradually add the stock, stirring to produce a sauce about the thickness of double cream. Taste, add salt and pepper, and serve with plain roast lamb or mutton.

Cumberland Sauce

A delicious sauce for cold ham or game. It appears to have no links with the county of that name, and a legend associating it with the royal title of the Duke of Cumberland appears to be just that – a legend. The base of redcurrant jelly and wine is reminiscent of 18th-century sauces for venison, but the first recognisable recipe was given (under a different name) by Alexis Soyer in 1853. It seems to have been the French chef Georges Auguste Escoffier who popularised the recipe and made it a commercial success in the 19th century.

serves
4–6

zest of 1 orange (preferably unwaxed),
    cut in thin strips
zest of 1 lemon (preferably unwaxed),
    cut in thin strips

4 tablespoons redcurrant jelly
4 tablespoons port
1 teaspoon smooth Dijon mustard
a pinch of ground ginger

Put the orange and lemon zest in a small bowl, then cover with boiling water and leave to blanch for 3–4 minutes. Drain well.

Melt the jelly in a small pan, stirring to smooth out any lumps. Add the port and mix well. Stir in the zest, the mustard and a little ginger. Taste and add a little more mustard or ginger if desired. Allow to cool before serving with cold meat.

Apple Sauce

Apple sauce is a traditional accompaniment for pork and goose. It is very simple to make: peel and core 2 large Bramley apples, then cut into small pieces. Cook gently in a small pan with just enough water to prevent them from sticking. Stir frequently. Once they have become a purée, add about 3 teaspoons of sugar, or to taste.

Caramelised Apples

These are good served with pork, goose or duck. If serving with duck, add a little grated orange zest at the end. The apples must be a firm-fleshed type that will keep their shape when cooked.

serves
4–6

30g (1oz) unsalted butter
3 large apples (Cox's or a dryish,
    aromatic eating apple), peeled,
    cored and sliced, but not too thinly

a piece of star anise (optional)
1 dessertspoon cider vinegar
2 tablespoons sugar

Melt the butter in a heavy frying pan and add the apple slices, and the star anise if using. Cook gently, stirring frequently, until the apple is softening and has become slightly transparent. Add the cider vinegar, then the sugar and continue to cook until the apple begins to caramelise. Serve tepid.

Sage and Onion Stuffing

This recipe – suitable for pork, goose or duck – was considered old-fashioned by the 1840s. It was also thought too overpowering by Victorian cooks, although Eliza Acton remarked that some people always liked it with leg of pork (which was stuffed at the knuckle end). It has outlived Victorians and remains one of the most iconic mixtures in the English kitchen. In her otherwise excellent recipe on which the one below is based, Mrs Roundell in *Mrs Roundell's Practical Cookery Book* (1898), suggested that a very few well-blanched sage leaves were sufficient. We are accustomed to much bigger flavours, so I have added a few more and omitted the blanching. A mixture based on one onion is about the right amount for stuffing a duck; double it for a goose.

serves 4–6

1 large onion, peeled
12 fresh sage leaves, washed
60g (2½oz) stale breadcrumbs
20g (¾oz) unsalted butter, cut in small pieces (or beef suet for a traditional mixture)

1 medium egg, beaten
½ teaspoon salt
a little freshly ground black pepper

Put the onion in a pan, cover with boiling water and simmer for 20–30 minutes, or until tender. Drain. Once it is cool enough to handle, cut it into quarters. Put it in a food processor with the sage and chop (but don't reduce it to a purée), or chop together by hand until fairly fine. Stir in the breadcrumbs, butter and enough egg to bind lightly, then stir in the seasoning (don't use the processor, which makes the mixture too runny).

Use to stuff a boned and rolled pork roast or a bird, or press into a greased dish and bake along with the roast for the last 30 minutes of cooking time.

Boulangère Potatoes

A dish of French origin, popularised in Britain during the love affair with French food in the mid-20th century. Marcel Boulestin gave an early version in his book *Simple French Cooking for English Homes* (1930). It is similar to *tiesen nionod*, a Welsh dish of onions and potatoes baked together like a gratin.

serves
4–6

2 large onions, peeled and thinly
   sliced
unsalted butter, for frying and for
   greasing the dish

about 750g (1lb 10oz) baking potatoes,
   peeled
150ml (5fl oz) well-flavoured stock
salt and pepper

Preheat the oven to 180–190°C, 350–375°F, Gas mark 4–5. Fry the onions gently in butter to soften them, but don't let them colour (they can be blanched in boiling water if you prefer). Slice the potatoes thinly.

Grease a shallow ovenproof dish with butter and arrange the potatoes and onions in layers, seasoning well as you go. Finish with a neat layer of overlapping potato slices. Dot with butter and pour in the stock; it should come almost to the top of the dish.

Bake in the oven until the potatoes are soft and the surface nicely browned. A little extra (hot) stock or water can be added during cooking if the dish seems to be drying out, but this dish is better for not swimming in liquid.

Mashed Potatoes

I can't remember where I first came across this version, but I think it was in a 19th-century book and the writer stated that it was the way the French made mashed potato.

**serves
4**

500g (1lb 2oz) potatoes
30g (1oz) unsalted butter
salt and pepper

Peel the potatoes, then cut into chunks and boil as usual. When tender, do not pour the cooking water down the sink, but drain it into a jug.

Add the butter to the potatoes and season with salt and pepper. Mash the potatoes, adding a little of the reserved cooking water and continuing to mash, adding more cooking water if necessary, or butter if you want, until you feel they have achieved the right consistency.

Potatoes Roast in Cream and Herbs

This is not a traditional method for roasting potatoes, but it is good with just about any meat, especially game.

serves 4–6

2–3 fresh rosemary sprigs about 6cm (2½in) long
8–10 fresh sage leaves
12 fresh thyme sprigs
1–2 garlic cloves, peeled

750g (1lb 10oz) potatoes, peeled and cut in 2cm (¾in) chunks
200ml (7fl oz) double cream
1 teaspoon salt
freshly ground black pepper

Preheat the oven to 200°C, 400°F, Gas mark 6.

Strip the leaves off the rosemary and chop them together with the sage, thyme and garlic. Mix the potatoes, cream, chopped herb mixture, salt and some pepper. Put them in an ovenproof dish or small roasting tin that holds them comfortably in a shallow layer.

Cook for about 30 minutes, stirring once or twice. By the end of this time, they should be tender (give them a little longer if not), and the cream should be thick, clinging to the potatoes, and lightly flecked with gold on the surface.

Roast Potatoes

Roast potatoes are a defining element of 'a proper roast'. King Edward, a potato variety with almost iconic status in Britain, probably has the best flavour, and can develop a fantastic crisp crust and melting interior. Wilja and Desirée are also good; Cara and Romano should produce reasonable results.

serves 4–6

1kg (2¼lb) potatoes
about 50g (2oz) fat for roasting,
    such as beef or pork dripping
salt

The oven needs to be hot – 200–220°C, 400–425°F, Gas mark 6–7. Peel the potatoes. Leave small ones whole, and cut large ones into smaller pieces (3–4 each). Put them in a pan, just cover with cold water, and bring to the boil. Boil for 5–7 minutes. Tip them into a colander and drain well.

Put the fat in a roasting tin and place in the oven to melt and get very hot. Take it out and add the potatoes. (Wear oven gloves and an apron in case the fat spits – it should be hot enough to sizzle satisfactorily.) Turn the potatoes well in the hot fat, sprinkle with salt, and roast for 40–50 minutes. In a gas oven, put the potatoes at the top. Turn once or twice during cooking, and add a little more salt each time.

Cabbage

serves
4

1 pointed cabbage or Savoy cabbage
about 15g (½oz) unsalted butter,
    bacon fat or olive oil

a few juniper berries, bruised
1–2 tablespoons cider vinegar
salt

Trim the cabbage leaves of their central stalk, wash and shred the leaves. Put them in a pan with a well-fitting lid. The water clinging to the leaves after washing should be enough, or add 2–3 tablespoons. Add the butter, juniper berries and a little salt. Put the lid on the pan and put it on the lowest heat for about 15 minutes. Look occasionally to make sure that the cabbage isn't drying up; add a small amount of water if it is. When just tender, add the cider vinegar, mix well and serve.

Red Cabbage

serves
6

1 generous tablespoon goose,
    pork or bacon fat, or oil
1 medium onion, peeled
    and roughly chopped
1–2 apples, preferably sourish ones,
    peeled, cored and chopped
1 small red cabbage, quartered,
    stem removed, finely sliced

2–3 tablespoons cider vinegar
2 tablespoons light pale brown sugar
4–5 cloves, bruised
5cm (2in) cinnamon stick
1 piece of orange zest (preferably
    unwaxed) about 5 x 2cm (2 x 1in)
1 teaspoon salt
freshly ground black pepper

Preheat the oven to 140°C, 275°F, Gas mark 1. Heat the fat in an ovenproof casserole and fry the onion until translucent. Stir in the apples, then the cabbage, and fry lightly for a few minutes. Add the other ingredients and stir well. Cover and transfer to the oven for about 1½ hours. This can be cooked on the hob, but the heat must be very low – and stir frequently, adding a little more water from time to time if it shows signs of drying up.

Roast Parsnips

This is a root that goes well with roast beef. Parsnips are considered to be at their best in winter, after the first frosts – freezing temperatures convert some of the starch in the living roots into sugar, and this caramelises when they are cooked. Look for ones that are fresh and firm; flabby parsnips don't cook well.

serves
4–6

about 50g (2oz) fat for roasting,
   such as dripping from beef
   or pork or lard
about 500g (1–1½lb) parsnips
salt

The method for cooking these is similar to that for Roast Potatoes (see page 212). Wash and trim the parsnips and scrape off the skin with a peeler. Cut, on the diagonal, into slices about 5mm (¼in) thick. They can be parboiled for about 5 minutes, but if they are good and fresh, this isn't necessary. Put the fat in a roasting tin in a hot oven at 220°C, 425°F, Gas mark 7.

Drain the parsnips well if parboiled, then tip into the hot fat (protect your hands with oven gloves). Turn them around in the fat, sprinkle with a little salt, and roast for 10 minutes. Turn the heat down to 190°C, 375°F, Gas mark 5, and cook for another 20–30 minutes, stirring occasionally so that they develop nicely browned surfaces. Drain well before serving.

Ragoo of Onions and Mushrooms

'Ragoo' was the 18th-century English cook's phonetic rendition of the French *ragoût*. Complex mixtures requiring two or three different meaty stocks, these dishes were all the rage at the time. They were used as sauces and garnishes, or could be dishes in their own right. This one is good with white meat poultry of all sorts – and can also be served with beef, mutton or game. A good meaty stock based on chicken or veal, plus some ham, bacon or gammon, is essential.

serves
4

2 tablepoons olive oil

1 small onion, peeled and very finely chopped

1 celery stick, trimmed and very finely chopped

1 medium carrot, trimmed and very finely chopped

100g (4oz) lean unsmoked bacon or gammon, very finely chopped

400ml (14fl oz) well-flavoured stock

a bouquet garni of fresh parsley, thyme, marjoram (optional)

400g (14oz) shallots or very small onions, peeled

200g (7oz) button mushrooms, trimmed

salt and pepper

Heat the oil in a saucepan. Add the onion, celery and carrot and fry briskly, stirring frequently until the vegetables begin to caramelise and turn golden brown at the edges. Add the bacon and continue to fry for another 5–10 minutes. Any trimmings from the mushrooms can be added too. Pour in the stock, then add the bouquet garni. Once the mixture has come to the boil, turn it to the lowest possible simmer and leave to cook until reduced by about half.

Put the shallots and mushrooms in a clean pan. Strain the reduced stock over them, pressing so that all the flavoursome juices pass through (but don't rub any of the solids through). Continue to cook very gently, stirring from time to time. By the time the onions are tender (about 45 minutes), the stock should be reduced to a few spoonfuls of thick, slightly syrupy liquid, just coating the vegetables. Taste and adjust the seasoning.

Crisp Fried Browned Onions

Useful as a garnish for all sorts of leftover meat and potato dishes, and good in cold beef sandwiches (see page 35). It may take a couple of goes to master this, but it's worth the effort.

**serves
2–4**

sunflower oil, for frying
1 large onion, peeled, halved
    lengthways and sliced very thinly

Line a plate or small tray with a few sheets of kitchen paper. Heat a layer of oil about 1cm (½in) deep in a frying pan (a heavy cast-iron one is best). Add the onions and regulate the heat so that they cook fairly fast. Partially cover the pan, so that there is a small gap for steam to escape. You will need to remove the lid and stir them fairly frequently, to make sure they cook evenly. Don't let them brown patchily.

When the onions start to look shrunken and are beginning to brown, leave the lid off and stir constantly. They should begin to brown quite rapidly; at this point, watch them closely. You want them to be brown, not burned. When they begin to change colour to a deeper, caramel brown, turn off the heat and remove them immediately with a slotted spoon. Scatter them over the kitchen paper to absorb any remaining oil.

Watercress Salad

A salad of watercress has a long history of accompanying roast birds at table. Served with duck, it usually had orange segments added, but if pomegranates are available, I think they are better.

serves
4

2 bunches of watercress,
  washed and picked over
the seeds of ½ pomegranate
  (or use the segments of 2 oranges –
  cut off the pith with a small,
  sharp knife)

For the dressing
scant 1 teaspoon smooth
  Dijon mustard
1 tablespoon wine vinegar
4–5 tablespoons olive oil
salt and pepper

For the dressing, mix the mustard and vinegar together, then season to taste. Stir in the oil. Toss the watercress with the dressing, then scatter with the pomegranate or orange and serve at once.

Puréed Brussels Sprouts

During the early 1980s, it seemed that all vegetables had to be served as purées, a fashion derived from the then influential French *nouvelle cuisine*. They have mostly had their moment and gone, but Brussels sprouts are good done this way and go very well with game birds.

serves
4

500g (1lb 2oz) Brussels sprouts,
  trimmed
125ml (4fl oz) single cream
salt and pepper

Cook the sprouts in boiling water until tender. Drain well. Process with the cream and add seasoning to taste. Don't overdo the processing – you should be left with a beautiful pale-green purée, lightly flecked with darker green, like a piece of jade.

Baked Puddings

Apple Cobs

Also known as Bomdard'd Apples or Apple Dumplings. In the original recipe the dumplings were boiled, but here they are baked. Use a really good-quality cooking apple that will go soft and puffy when cooked. You can use shortcrust or puff pastry instead of suet-crust pastry if you want a less rich pudding.

serves
6

350g (12oz) self-raising flour
pinch of salt
175g (6oz) suet
50g (1¾oz) caster sugar
about 150ml (¼ pint) ice-cold water
6 medium Bramley apples

2 tablespoons mincemeat
6 cloves
water or milk for brushing
1 egg white, beaten
3 tablespoons clotted cream
   (optional)

Sieve the flour and salt together into a mixing bowl. Mix in the suet and stir in half the sugar. Add just sufficient water to mix to a soft but not sticky dough. Turn out on to a lightly floured board and divide into 6 equal pieces. Roll out each piece thinly into a square large enough to encase an apple.

Peel and core the apples and place one in the centre of each pastry square. Fill each apple centre with mincemeat and top with a clove. Brush the edge of each pastry square with a little water or milk, draw up the corners to meet over the centre of each apple and press the edges firmly together. Turn upside down, and place on a greased baking tray. Roll out the pastry trimmings to make small leaves to decorate the dumplings, then brush all over with the egg white and sprinkle with the remaining sugar.

Bake in the centre of a preheated oven at 200°C (400°F, Gas mark 6) for 30 minutes or until golden brown. Remove from the oven and leave to stand for a few minutes on a warm serving dish. Cut a hole in the top of each dumpling and spoon in some clotted cream, or serve with Custard.

Nottingham Pudding

Also known as Apple-In-and-Out, this pudding is a combination of apple and batter, dating back to medieval days when dried fruits, spices and candied peel were put in a batter pudding and served with joints of meat. This tradition has continued in the north of England, where any leftovers are served after the meal with melted butter and treacle, lemon juice and sugar or warmed honey and cinnamon.

**serves
4–6**

115g (4oz) plain flour
pinch of salt
1 large egg
150ml (¼ pint) full-cream milk
150ml (¼ pint) water
450g (1lb) cooking apples

40g (1½oz) butter
zest of ½ lemon
½ teaspoon ground cinnamon
70g (2½oz) soft brown sugar
40g (1½oz) margarine

Sieve the flour and salt together into a basin and make a well in the centre. Break the egg into the well and stir to mix with the flour. Gradually add half the milk and water, beating well with a wooden spoon until the batter is smooth and creamy. Add the remaining liquid, beating with a rotary or electric whisk to keep the batter smooth and light. Leave to stand in a cool place for about 30 minutes.

Peel, core and slice the apples. Melt the butter in a heavy frying pan, add the apples, lemon zest, cinnamon and sugar, cover and cook gently until the apples are just tender.

Put the margarine in a 19cm (7½in) square baking tin and heat near the top of a preheated oven at 220°C (425°F, Gas mark 7) until the fat is smoking. Remove from the oven and carefully add the apple mixture and pour the batter over. Return to the oven for about 20 minutes, then reduce the temperature to 190°C (375°F, Gas mark 5) for a further 20–25 minutes or until the batter is firm and golden brown (this batter pudding will not rise as much as a Yorkshire pudding, because of the fruit it contains).

Mother Eve's Pudding

Traditionally made with tempting apples under a sponge topping, hence the name! However, you can use any fruit and the flavourings can be varied accordingly by adding spices or orange zest. The Georgian recipe for this pudding was made with suet and included currants as well as the apples. It was also boiled rather than baked.

serves
6

600g (1lb 5oz) cooking apples
85g (3oz) caster sugar
zest of 1 lemon
2 cloves
1 tablespoon water
115g (4oz) salted butter

115g (4oz) caster sugar
2 eggs
¼ teaspoon vanilla extract
115g (4oz) self-raising flour
1 tablespoon warm water
caster sugar for dredging

Butter a 1.2 litre (2 pint) ovenproof dish. Peel, core and slice the apples thinly and place in a heavy saucepan with the sugar, lemon zest, cloves and water. Heat over gentle heat for a few minutes until just tender. Turn into the prepared dish and leave to cool.

Cream butter and sugar together in a mixing bowl until pale and fluffy. Beat eggs and add gradually to creamed mixture, beating well after each addition. Beat in the vanilla extract, and gently fold sieved flour into creamed mixture. Stir in warm water to make a soft dropping consistency and spread evenly over apples.

Bake in the centre of a preheated oven at 190°C (375°F, Gas mark 5) for about 45 minutes, or until well risen and golden brown (test with a fine skewer, which should come out clean). Serve hot or cold, dredged with caster sugar.

Apple & Almond Pudding

Substitute 115g (4oz) ground almonds for self-raising flour and continue as before. Serve hot or cold with pouring cream.

Gingerbread & Pear Upside-down Pudding

This was a popular pudding in Victorian days and looks very attractive. You can bake it in a round or square tin.

serves 6

50g (1¾oz) butter
140g (5oz) soft brown sugar
3 firm pears
6 glacé cherries
6 walnut halves
115g (4oz) margarine
115g (4oz) black treacle
115g (4oz) golden syrup
225g (8oz) plain flour

¼ teaspoon salt
pinch of ground cloves
2 teaspoons ground cinnamon
2 teaspoons ground ginger
¼ teaspoon grated nutmeg
1 level teaspoon bicarbonate of soda
150ml (¼ pint) warm
   full-cream milk
2 eggs

Line the bottom and sides of a 20cm (8in) round cake tin with buttered greaseproof paper. Melt the butter in a saucepan over gentle heat, add 70g (2½oz) brown sugar and stir for a few minutes until dissolved. Pour into the bottom of the tin. Peel, halve and core the pears and put a glacé cherry in the centre of each pear half. Arrange the pears in a circle cut-side down on the butter-and-sugar mixture with stalk ends facing the centre of the tin. Place walnut halves, cut-side down, between the pears.

Put margarine, black treacle, golden syrup and remaining brown sugar in a saucepan and melt over a low heat. Sieve flour, salt and spices together into a mixing bowl. Dissolve soda in warm milk. Beat eggs and add to milk mixture when it has cooled a little. Make a well in the centre of the dry ingredients and pour in melted treacle mixture, followed by egg mixture. Stir together and beat thoroughly until a smooth batter is formed. Pour carefully over the pears and walnuts. Bake in the centre of a preheated oven at 180°C (350°F, Gas mark 4) for 40–50 minutes or until well risen and firm (test with a skewer; it should come out clean). Remove from the oven and allow to shrink a little before turning out on to a warmed serving plate. Take great care when peeling off greaseproof paper. Serve warm with cream or custard.

Plum & Cinnamon Crumble

Crumbles can be varied, not just by using seasonal fruit but also by changing the crumble topping, adding porridge oats (as here), dessicated coconut, chopped nuts, different spices and so on. Classic combinations such as rhubarb and ginger, apple and cinnamon, gooseberry and elderflower, can always be relied on. This particular recipe was given to me by a good friend, who is chef at Cotehele, a medieval house belonging to the National Trust on the banks of the River Tamar, in Cornwall. He cooks the crumble in individual dishes under the grill.

serves 4

600g (1 lb 5oz) English plums, stoned
50g (1¾oz) light brown sugar
½ teaspoon ground cinnamon

for the topping
40g (1½oz) butter, cut in small pieces
55g (2oz) plain flour
1/2 teaspoon cinnamon
40g (1½oz) light brown sugar
55g (2oz) porridge oats

Poach the plums with the sugar and cinnamon and a very little water until just tender. Remove from the heat and tip into a buttered ovenproof baking dish.

Rub the butter into the flour and cinnamon sieved together, into a mixing bowl until the mixture resembles breadcrumbs. Stir in the sugar and oats.

Sprinkle evenly over the plums and bake in a preheated oven at 180°C (350°F, Gas mark 4) for about 25 minutes, or until golden brown. Remove from the oven and leave to cool a little. Eat warm and serve with custard, ice cream or cream.

Damson Cobbler

This pudding presumably takes its name from the scone topping, which does look rather like cobblestones. You can either cut out dough into circles and place them round the edges of the dish, overlapping each other, or you can lay the dough over like a pie crust and cut it into squares – either way, it is a delicious and economical pudding. Many fruits can be used instead of damsons – plums, greengages, blackcurrants, blackberries, apples, rhubarb, bilberries and gooseberries. This particular recipe is made in Cumbria from local damsons.

serves
6

900g (2lb) damsons
250g (9oz) caster sugar
150ml (¼ pint) water
225g (8oz) self-raising flour
pinch of salt
55g (2oz) butter
1 egg
1–2 tablespoons milk
granulated sugar for sprinkling

Wash the damsons and cook slowly in a heavy saucepan with 225g (8oz) sugar and the water until just tender. Remove the stones and turn into a buttered ovenproof dish. Leave to cool.

Sieve the flour and salt together into a mixing bowl. Stir in the remaining sugar and rub in the butter. Beat the egg and add to the mixture with enough milk to make a soft dough. Roll out on a lightly floured board to about 1cm (½in) thick. Cut out the dough into rounds with a 5cm (2in) cutter and arrange in a ring around the edge of the dish of fruit with the rounds overlapping each other. Brush the scone topping with a little milk, and bake near the top of a preheated oven at 220°C (425°F, Gas mark 7) for 10 minutes. Reduce the oven temperature to 190°C (375°F, Gas mark 5). Sprinkle the top generously with granulated sugar and bake for a further 5–10 minutes until well risen and golden brown.

Lemon Pudding

This lovely pudding is based on a very old recipe which was baked in a dish lined with puff pastry. By whisking egg whites and adding just before baking, the pudding will be very light. You may need to cover with greaseproof paper if the top is getting brown too quickly before the underneath has set. This pudding separates out during cooking into a tangy custard layer with a featherlight sponge topping. An orange or lime pudding can be made in the same way.

serves
4–6

100g (3½oz) butter, softened
175g (6oz) caster sugar
zest and juice of 4 lemons
4 eggs, separated
125ml (4fl oz) full-cream milk
50g (1¾oz) plain flour

Cream the butter and sugar together until white and fluffy, then beat in the lemon zest and juice. Beat the egg yolks into the creamed mixture very gradually. When the mixture is very light, beat in the milk. Fold in the sieved flour.

Whisk the egg whites until they are firm and stand in peaks. Fold them gently into the lemon mixture, then pour into a buttered 20cm (8in) soufflé dish. Place the dish in a roasting tin and pour hot water into the tin until it comes halfway up the sides of the dish.

Bake in the centre of a preheated oven at 180°C (350°F, Gas mark 4), for about 45 minutes, until the top is golden brown and the pudding has risen. Serve warm, or cold with cream.

Cherry Batter

This famous pudding from Kent has been eaten at cherry feasts and fairs since the 13th century, but probably the idea of combining cherries with batter came to the UK with the Normans. This dish is a reminder that Kent was one of the first counties to be colonised by the invaders. Kent's famous juicy black morello cherries, said to be the best black cherries in the world, should be used to make this delicious pud, but drained tinned black cherries can be used out of season.

serves
6

50g (1¾oz) plain flour
pinch of salt
50g (1¾oz) caster sugar
2 eggs
300ml (½ pint) single-
   or full-cream milk

1 tablespoon cherry brandy or
   a few drops of vanilla essence
25g (1oz) melted butter
450g (1lb) ripe black cherries,
   stoned
icing sugar for dredging

Sieve the flour and salt together into a bowl. Stir in the caster sugar. Beat the eggs and blend gradually into flour mixture. Warm the milk and add slowly to the flour mixture beating vigorously to make a smooth light batter. Stir in cherry brandy or vanilla essence and whisk in melted butter. Put aside to rest while you stone the cherries.

Generously butter a shallow 600ml (1 pint) ovenproof porcelain dish or a 20cm (8in) flan tin. Spread the prepared cherries over the bottom of the dish or tin and carefully pour over the batter. Dot with a few tiny pieces of butter and bake in the centre of a preheated oven at 200°C (400°F, Gas mark 6) for 20 minutes, then reduce the temperature to 190°C (375°F, Gas mark 5) and cook for a further 20 minutes or until the batter is well risen and golden, but still creamy inside. Serve warm, generously dredged with sieved icing sugar and with whipped cream or custard. If you want to serve the pudding cold, remove from the dish or tin and serve with either pouring or whipped cream.

Apricot Amber Pudding

Traditionally, an Amber Pudding was made with apples and baked in a puff-pastry case. It is a very old-fashioned sweet dating back to the 18th century, and can be made with many other fruits such as apples, rhubarb, gooseberries, blackberries, blackcurrants or plums.

serves
6

175g (6oz) shortcrust pastry
450g (1lb) fresh apricots
about 150g (5½oz)
    caster sugar
1 teaspoon lemon juice

25g (1oz) unsalted butter
2 eggs, separated
pinch of salt
crystallized apricot and
    angelica to decorate

Preheat the oven to 200°C (400°C, Gas mark 6), with a large baking sheet in the oven to warm up as well. Roll out the pastry thinly and use to line a buttered 20cm (8in) shallow ovenproof dish. Chill in the refrigerator for 30 minutes. Prick the base and line with baking paper and baking beans. Place in the oven on the hot baking sheet and bake blind for about 10 minutes, then remove the baking parchment and beans and cook for about another 10 minutes to dry out the inside without browning the pastry.

Meanwhile, wash and stone the apricots, then poach in a little water until tender. Rub the fruit through a plastic sieve, then sweeten with about 40g (1½oz) sugar or to taste, adding the lemon juice. Stir in the butter, and beat in the egg yolks. Leave on one side to cool.

Pour the cooled apricot mixture into the cooked pastry case and cook for 20 minutes in the preheated oven at 200°C (400°F, Gas mark 6).

Whisk the egg whites with the salt until stiff, but not dry. Add 55g (2oz) caster sugar and whisk until stiff again. Fold in another 55g (2oz) sugar gently. Reduce the oven temperature to 180°C (350°F, Gas mark 4). Pile the meringue on top of the apricot mixture and spread out, making sure that it touches the edges of the pastry. Dredge with extra caster sugar and bake in the centre of the oven for 20 minutes, or until the meringue is crisp and very lightly browned. Serve warm or cold with whipped cream and decorated with pieces of crystallized apricot and candied angelica, if you wish.

Rich Bakewell Pudding

There are several 'original' recipes in Derbyshire for this famous pudding, but generally it is accepted that it was probably first made by a cook at the Rutland Arms in Bakewell two hundred years ago. The original recipe was made in a special oval tin 7.5cm (3in) deep and 15cm (6in) wide and had a thick layer of preserved fruit, such as peaches or apricots, and strips of candied citron or orange peel spread over the pastry. A custard made with eggs, butter and sugar and flavoured with what the Bakewellians call 'lemon brandy' (brandy flavoured with lemon zest) was poured on top of the preserved fruit and the pudding was baked. Ratafia or almond flavouring is more commonly used now, and flaky or rich shortcrust pastry can be used instead of shortcrust.

**serves
6**

175g (6oz) shortcrust pastry
3 heaped tablespoons homemade or
   good-quality apricot jam
25g (1oz) candied peel, chopped
3 eggs
115g (4oz) caster sugar

115g (4oz) unsalted butter
½ teaspoon vanilla extract or
   ratafia flavouring
1 tablespoon brandy
115g (4oz) ground almonds
sieved icing sugar for dredging

Roll out the pastry and use to line a buttered 20cm (8in) oval pie dish. Chill, then bake blind in the usual way. Spread the jam evenly over the cooled pastry case and sprinkle with the peel.

Beat eggs and sugar together until pale and thick. Melt the butter and run into egg mixture. Beat together well. Stir in vanilla essence or ratafia and brandy. Fold in ground almonds. Pour the mixture over the jam and candied peel in the pastry case. Bake in the centre of the preheated oven at 180°C (350°F, Gas mark 4), for about 30 minutes or until the filling is set and golden brown. Dredge with sieved icing sugar and serve hot, warm or cold with pouring cream.

Jam Roly-Poly

This popular pudding used to be boiled in a cloth or shirtsleeve, but baking gives the pastry a lovely crisp crust which is usually more popular with children. Mincemeat or golden syrup can be used instead of jam.

serves
4–6

225g (8oz) self-raising flour
1 teaspoon mixed spice (optional)
pinch of salt
115g (4oz) suet
about 8 tablespoons water

4–5 tablespoons good-quality
  jam, warmed
milk, for brushing
1 egg, beaten, to glaze
caster sugar for sprinkling

Sieve flour, spice (if using) and salt together into a mixing bowl. Stir in the suet and add just enough water to mix to a soft, but not sticky, dough. Turn out on to a lightly floured board and roll into a rectangle about 20 x 30cm (8 x 12in). Spread evenly with warm jam leaving a 1cm (½in) border all the way around. Fold this border over the jam and brush with milk. Roll up fairly loosely and press the edges of the dough together to seal them. Put in a lightly buttered roasting tin and brush with beaten egg. Sprinkle with caster sugar.

Bake in the centre of a preheated oven at 200°C (400°F, Gas mark 6), with the tin propped up so that the roly-poly rolls into one end, which helps to keep its shape. Cook for 35–40 minutes or until golden brown.

Serve warm, sprinkled with extra caster sugar and custard.

Roly-poly with Blueberries

Make the roly-poly as before, but fill with 300g (10½oz) fresh blueberries mixed with 1 tablespoon flour, 4 tablespoons caster sugar and juice of 1 lemon or lime. Try other seasonal soft fruits and serve with custard, ice cream or thick cream.

Bread & Butter Pudding

Bread and Butter Pudding was in the recipe books by the 1720s, when it was made of freshly sliced and buttered bread with currants, beaten eggs and nutmeg. It was only in Victorian times that it became a means of putting stale bread to good use. Since then it has become a British institution and there are dozens of versions. Modern recipes sometimes add fresh or poached fruit, marmalade, apricot jam or chocolate and use brioche, fruit loaf, panettone and croissants. I love a Bread and Butter Pudding with a high proportion of rich custard to bread.

serves 6

300ml (½ pint) full-cream or Jersey milk
300ml (½ pint) double cream
1 vanilla pod, split in half lengthways
4–6 slices cut from a good-quality white sandwich loaf

about 100g (3½oz) butter, softened
55g (2oz) sultanas, soaked in hot water
25g (1oz) candied peel, chopped
3 large eggs
about 70g (2½oz) caster sugar
freshly grated nutmeg
icing sugar for dredging

Slowly heat the milk and cream with the vanilla pod, including its scraped-out seeds, until boiling point is just reached. Take off the heat and leave to cool a little.

Remove the crusts from the bread and butter generously. Cut each slice into 4 triangles, then arrange, overlapping in the base of a well-buttered 1.5 litre (2¾ pint) ovenproof dish. Sprinkle with the soaked and drained sultanas and peel.

Whisk the eggs with the sugar, then pour into a jug with the strained milk and cream mixture. Taste and add more sugar, if you wish. Whisk again, then carefully pour evenly over the bread, making sure that each triangle gets a good soaking (add more milk if the liquid doesn't cover the bread). Grate plenty of nutmeg over the surface, cover and leave to soak for at least 2 hours, preferably overnight, in the refrigerator. When ready to cook, place the dish in a roasting tin filled with hot water to the level of the top of the custard.

Bake in a preheated oven at 150°C (300°F, Gas mark 2) for 1–1¼ hours until just set and golden (after 30 minutes cooking time, dredge with icing sugar to crisp up the top). Rest for 20 minutes before serving. No extra cream is really necessary because the custard is very rich and delicious.

Old-fashioned Bread Pud

In Plymouth, this very old pudding is called Nelson's Cake after the great man who was obviously a lover of it. It is also particularly popular in East Anglia, where Nelson was born. The original version would have been boiled but it is now more commonly baked. Individual bread puddings were fashionable in Georgian times – they were baked in buttered teacups.

serves
4

225g (8oz) stale white or brown
   bread, with crusts removed
300ml (½ pint) milk
2 tablespoons brandy (optional)
50g (1¾oz) melted butter or suet
50g (1¾oz) soft brown sugar
2 level teaspoons mixed spice

1 egg, beaten
175g (6oz) mixed dried fruit
zest of 1 lemon
zest of ½ orange
freshly grated nutmeg
caster sugar for sprinkling

Break the bread into small pieces and put in a mixing bowl. Pour over the milk and brandy, if using, stir well and leave to soak for at least 30 minutes.

Add the melted butter or suet, sugar, spice and egg then, using a fork, beat out any lumps. Stir in the dried fruit and grated lemon and orange zest, then turn the mixture into a buttered 1.2 litre (2 pint) ovenproof dish. Grate a little fresh nutmeg over the top.

Bake in a preheated oven at 180°C (350°F, Gas mark 4) for 1¼–1½ hours until nicely brown on top. Serve hot, sprinkled with caster sugar and with custard.

Old-fashioned Iced Bread Pud
Make as before, but remove from the oven after 1 hour. Cover with meringue made from 2 egg whites and 115g (4oz) caster sugar. Put back in the oven and cook for a further 20 minutes, or until the meringue is crisp and lightly browned.

Hollygog Pudding

This is a golden syrupy roly-poly which is baked in milk. It was first made in the Oxfordshire village of Kiddington, where it has been passed down among farming families.

serves
4–6

225g (8oz) plain flour
pinch of salt
115g (4oz) butter
about 3 tablespoons cold water
4 tablespoons golden syrup, warmed
about 300ml (½ pint) full-cream milk

Sieve the flour and salt into a mixing bowl and rub the fat into the flour until the mixture resembles breadcrumbs. Add water to form a stiff dough. Roll out into a rectangular strip, spread with syrup and roll up like a Swiss roll.

Put in a well-buttered oval ovenproof dish and pour over enough milk to come halfway up the side of the pudding. Bake in a preheated oven at 200°C (400°F, Gas mark 6) for 40–45 minutes.

Serve hot in slices with cream, or custard.

Icky Sticky Toffee Sponge

A top favourite with most people, the original recipe for this pudding probably dates back to the 1930s. It was made famous in the 1960s by the late great Francis Coulson, chef and proprietor of the Sharrow Bay Country House Hotel in Ullswater, Cumbria.

serves
6–8

for the sponge
50g (1¾oz) butter
175g (6oz) granulated sugar
175g (6oz) dates, stoned and chopped
300ml (½ pint) water
1 teaspoon bicarbonate of soda
2 large eggs
175g (6oz) self-raising flour
a few drops of vanilla extract

for the sauce
40g (1½oz) demerara sugar
1 tablespoon black treacle, golden
   syrup or honey
300ml (½ pint) double cream

To make the sponge, cream the butter and sugar together. Boil the chopped dates in the water for about 10 minutes or until soft, then add the bicarbonate of soda. Beat the eggs into the creamed mixture, followed by the sieved flour, dates, water and vanilla extract. Pour into a buttered 20cm (8in) round, loose-bottomed cake tin that is at least 7.5cm (3in) deep. Bake in a preheated oven at 180°C (350°F, Gas mark 4) for about 40 minutes, or until firm to the touch.

Meanwhile, make the sauce. Put the sugar and treacle in a pan and heat gently, stirring until the sugar has dissolved. Stir in the cream and bring to the boil. Remove from the heat and leave to stand until needed.

When the pudding is cooked, remove from the oven and leave for 5 minutes, then turn out on to a warm serving plate. Pour over the sauce. Put under the grill for a few minutes until the sauce bubbles, then serve with ice cream.

Chocolate Puddle Pudding

A firm family favourite, this pudding emerges from the oven with its own built-in sauce hidden under a layer of chocolate sponge. Its exact origin is vague although it has been around for years.

serves 4–6

for the pudding
115g (4oz) butter, softened
115g (4oz) soft light
   brown sugar
1 teaspoon vanilla extract
2 large eggs, beaten
85g (3oz) self-raising flour
25g (1oz) cocoa powder
a little milk

for the sauce
85g (3oz) light brown sugar
25g (1oz) cocoa powder
300ml (½ pint) full-cream milk

Preheat the oven to 180°C (350°F, Gas mark 4). Cream the butter and sugar together until light and fluffy. Beat in the vanilla extract, then gradually beat in the eggs.

Sieve the flour and cocoa together, then fold into the creamed mixture. Mix in just enough milk to give a soft dropping consistency. Spoon into a buttered 1.2 litre (2 pint) ovenproof dish.

For the sauce, mix the sugar and cocoa together and gradually beat in the milk. Pour evenly over the pudding mixture and bake for 40–60 minutes, or until just set in the centre. (If the pudding is a bit too soft in the centre, the sauce will be thin when you cut into the pudding, but if you overcook so that the pudding is very firm in the centre, the sauce will disappear. The centre should spring back when you press it lightly, with your fingertips.) Leave to stand for 5 minutes, before serving with ice cream or cream.

Pies, Tarts & Flans

Lemon Meringue Pie

serves
6

for the pastry
175g (6oz) plain flour
1 tablespoon icing sugar
115g (4oz) cold butter, cut in
    small pieces
1 egg yolk
about 1 tablespoon ice-cold water

for the filling
115g (4oz) caster sugar
2 level tablespoons cornflour

zest of 2 large lemons
125ml (4fl oz) lemon juice
juice of 1 small orange
85g (3oz) butter, cut in small pieces
3 egg yolks
1 whole egg

for the meringue
4 egg whites, at room temperature
225g (8oz) caster sugar
2 level teaspoons cornflour

To make the pastry, sieve the flour and icing sugar together into a mixing bowl. Lightly rub in the butter, then add the egg yolk and enough water to mix to a dough. Knead briefly into a smooth ball, then roll out and line a buttered 23cm (9in) loose-bottomed, fluted flan tin. Prick the base with a fork, line with foil and chill for 30 minutes to 1 hour or overnight. Put a baking sheet in the oven and preheat to 200°C (400°F, Gas mark 6). Bake blind in the usual way. Remove from the oven and set aside. Lower the oven to 180°C (350°F, Gas mark 4).

To make the filling, mix the sugar, cornflour and lemon zest in a medium saucepan. Strain and stir in the lemon juice gradually. Make the orange juice up to 200ml (7fl oz) with water and strain into the pan. Cook over a medium heat, stirring continuously, until thick and smooth. Once the mixture bubbles, remove from the heat and beat in the butter until melted. Beat the egg yolks and whole egg together, then add to the pan and return to the heat. Keep stirring vigorously for a few minutes until the mixture thickens and plops from the spoon. Remove from the heat and set aside.

Whisk the egg whites to soft peaks, then add half the sugar, a spoonful at a time, whisking between each addition without overbeating. Whisk in the cornflour, then add the rest of the sugar as before until smooth and glossy. Quickly reheat the filling and pour it into the pastry case. Immediately pile spoonfuls of meringue around the edge of the filling (if you start in the middle, the meringue may sink), then spread so it just touches the pastry (to anchor it and help stop it sliding). Pile the remaining meringue into the centre, spreading so that it touches the surface of the hot filling and starts to cook, then give it all a swirl. Return to the oven for 18–20 minutes until the meringue is crisp.

Remove from the oven and leave in the tin for 30 minutes, then remove and leave for at least another 30 minutes to 1 hour before serving. Eat the same day, or the meringue will be spoiled.

Mucky-mouth Pie

A traditional fruit pie from the north of England made with apples, bilberries and fresh mint. For many centuries the latter was thought to be aphrodisiac, but who knows whether northern housewives were aware of this? Certainly this pie was a favourite with their menfolk. The pastry lid is 'iced' in the traditional way, so the fruit needs to be on the sharp side. If you don't want to use bilberries, blackcurrants, blackberries, blueberries or damsons are all suitable.

serves 6

225g (8oz) shortcrust pastry

for the filling
2 large Bramley apples
450g (1lb) bilberries
a little caster sugar

2 tablespoons fresh mint, finely chopped

for the icing
1 large egg white
115g (4oz) icing sugar

Chill the pastry, then roll out half of it and use it to line a buttered 20cm (8in) pie plate. Prick the base of the pastry, then chill again.

Peel, core and slice the apples and cook them to a purée with a very little water. Mix with the bilberries and chopped mint. Sprinkle with a little sugar – not too much because of the sweet icing on top of the pie. Spoon the fruit mixture into the flan ring or pie plate and roll out the rest of the pastry to make a lid. Bake in a preheated oven at 200°C (400°F, Gas mark 6) for about 25 minutes, then remove from the oven and leave to cool slightly. Reduce the oven to 180°C (350°F, Gas mark 4).

To prepare the icing, whisk the egg white until very stiff, then whisk in the sieved icing sugar until the mixture stands in peaks. Spread thickly over the pie crust and put back in the oven for about 10 minutes, until the icing hardens and is very slightly browned. Serve warm with cream.

Royal Pie

In Elizabethan times a 'royal pye' was any savoury or sweet pie which was 'iced' with sugar and egg white, more like modern royal icing than meringue, which is a descendant. This particular Royal Pye is filled with mincemeat, apples and grapes and is ideal for serving at Christmas alongside, or instead of, the plum pudding. The rich shortcrust pastry was originally called 'biscuit crust'.

serves 6–8

175g (6oz) sweet shortcrust pastry
(see Chocolate and Prune Tart
page 182)

for the filling
450g (1lb) Cox's apples

115g (4oz) seedless green grapes
450g (1lb) homemade or good-quality
mincemeat
1–2 tablespoons brandy or sherry
2 egg whites
115g (4oz) caster sugar

After making your pastry, chill in the refrigerator for 30 minutes, then roll out and use to line a buttered 23cm (9in) flan tin. Chill again for about 15 minutes. Preheat the oven to 200°C (400°F, Gas mark 6) and bake blind in the usual way.

Peel, core and chop the apples. Halve the grapes if large. Mix the apples and grapes with the mincemeat, stir in the brandy or sherry, then spoon the mixture into the pastry case. Cook in the preheated oven at 190°C (375°F, Gas mark 5) for 30 minutes.

Whisk the egg whites until stiff and whisk in half the caster sugar until smooth and glossy. Gently fold in the remaining sugar and pile the meringue on top of the pie. Put back in the oven and bake for a further 15–20 minutes until meringue is crisp and lightly brown. Serve warm with cream.

Raspberries & Cream Tart

This delicious tart recipe is based on one which dates back to the 17th century. In the original, the highly spiced raspberries were set in an egg custard and cooked in a thin-lidded puff-pastry pie. Other soft fruits like strawberries, cherries, blueberries and bilberries are successful and almond pastry is delicious, although more difficult to handle.

serves
6–8

175g (6oz) sweet shortcrust pastry (see Chocolate and Prune Tart page 182, but add 2–3 drops of vanilla extract to the egg yolks)

for the filling
900g (2lb) fresh raspberries
about 115g (4oz) caster sugar
3 large eggs
1 level tablespoon cornflour
300ml (½ pint) single cream
1 tablespoon raspberry liqueur

After making and chilling the pastry, use it to line a buttered 25cm (10in) flan tin. Chill again for 15 minutes, then bake blind in the usual way (see Apricot Amber Pudding, page 32). Remove the pastry case from the oven and set aside to cool.

Reduce the oven temperature to 180°C (350°F, Gas mark 4). Fill the pastry case with raspberries and sprinkle them with 85g (3oz) caster sugar. Beat the eggs, remaining sugar and cornflour together until almost white. Stir in the cream and liqueur and taste for sweetness. Add more sugar if you wish. Pour the egg mixture over the raspberries and bake in the centre of the oven for 35–40 minutes, or until the custard has just set.

Serve warm with ice cream or cream.

Cherry & Brandy Dish Pie

Cherry pies and 'bumpers', or pasties, were baked and eaten at cherry-pie feasts to celebrate the harvesting of the fruit in the principal cherry-growing areas of England, such as Kent and Buckinghamshire.

serves 6

for the pastry
225g (8oz) plain flour
pinch of salt
115g (4oz) butter
25g (1oz) caster sugar
1 egg yolk
about 2 tablespoons
    ice-cold water

for the filling
900g (2lb) stoned cherries
about 115g (4oz) caster sugar
knob of butter
milk and caster sugar, for glazing
2 tablespoons cherry brandy
    or brandy
3 tablespoons double cream

Sieve the flour and salt together into a mixing bowl. Rub in the butter until the mixture resembles breadcrumbs. Stir in the caster sugar, egg yolk and enough cold water to mix to a firm dough. Knead lightly until smooth and chill for at least 30 minutes. Fill a 850ml (1½ pint) pie dish with stoned cherries, sprinkle with sugar and dot with butter.

Roll out the pastry on a lightly floured board and cover the dish of cherries. Flute the edges of pastry lid and make a couple of slits in the top to let out the steam. Decorate with pastry trimmings. Brush with milk and caster sugar. Bake in the centre of a preheated oven at 200°C (400°F, Gas mark 6) for 20 minutes, then reduce the heat to 190°C (375°F, Gas mark 5) and continue cooking for 20–25 minutes or until pastry is golden brown.

Remove from oven and cut neatly round the lid of the pie. Lift off carefully, and pour cherry brandy or brandy and cream over the fruit. Replace the pastry lid, dredge with extra caster sugar and return to the oven for 5 minutes. Serve hot with whipped or clotted cream.

Cumberland Rum Nicky

Small versions of this pie, similar to mince pies and called Rum Nickies, can also be made. It recalls the days in the 18th century when Whitehaven in Cumbria was one of the leading ports in the rum trade with the West Indies.

serves 6

for the pastry
225g (8oz) plain flour
pinch of salt
115g (4oz) butter
25g (1oz) caster sugar
1 egg yolk
2–3 tablespoons ice-cold water

for the filling
115g (4oz) chopped dates
50g (1¾oz) chopped preserved ginger
50g (1¾oz) butter
25g (1oz) caster sugar
2 tablespoons dark rum
icing sugar for dredging

Sieve the flour and salt together into a mixing bowl. Rub in the butter until mixture resembles breadcrumbs. Stir in the sugar. Add the egg yolk and enough ice-cold water to mix to a firm dough. Knead lightly until smooth. Chill for at least 30 minutes.

Roll out the pastry on a lightly floured board. Line a greased 20cm (8in) pie or ovenproof plate with half the pastry. Sprinkle over the chopped dates and ginger. Cream the butter and the sugar together until pale and fluffy. Beat in the rum gradually. Spread the mixture over the fruit in the pie plate. Cover with the remaining pastry, sealing the edges well. Make a couple of slits in the top of the pastry, flute the edges and decorate as you wish with pastry trimmings.

Bake in the centre of a preheated oven at 200°C (400°F, Gas mark 6) for 10–15 minutes and then reduce temperature to 180°C (350°F, Gas mark 4) for a further 25–30 minutes. Serve hot, dredged with icing sugar and with whipped or clotted cream..

Chocolate & Prune Tart

Chocolate was introduced into Britain in the mid-17th century from Mexico, where the Aztecs had mixed it with honey. It remained a luxury drink as long as the price of sugar was high, and was never as popular as coffee or tea. A pie with a chocolate filling like this would have been considered a great luxury.

serves 8–10

for the sweet shortcrust pastry
175g (6oz) plain flour
pinch of salt
85g (3oz) icing sugar
150g (5½oz) unsalted butter
2 small egg yolks, beaten

for the prune purée
300g (10½oz) stoned
   ready-to-eat prunes
2 tablespoons brandy

for the chocolate filling
100g (3½oz) good-quality plain
   chocolate (70% cocoa fat)
2 eggs, separated
300ml (½ pint) double cream
85g (3oz) caster sugar
sifted icing sugar, to dust

To make the pastry, sieve the flour with the salt and icing sugar into a bowl. Rub in the butter, then mix to a soft dough with the egg yolks. Knead very briefly, then wrap in clingfilm and chill in the refrigerator for 30 minutes. Roll out and use to line a buttered, 25cm (10in) flan tin. Bake blind..

Meanwhile, make the prune purée by simmering the prunes gently with barely enough water to cover, for 5–10 minutes or until very tender. Lift them out with a slotted spoon and process with the brandy and just enough of the juice to make a thick purée (about 3 tablespoonfuls). Spread over the base of the pastry case.

To make the chocolate filling, break the chocolate into pieces and place in a bowl, set over a pan of gently simmering water, making sure that the base of the bowl does not come into contact with the water. Remove the bowl as soon as the chocolate has melted and cool slightly, then beat in the egg yolks one by one. Lightly whip the cream and fold into the chocolate mixture. Whisk the egg whites until they form soft peaks, then sprinkle over the caster sugar and continue to whisk until glossy. Fold into the chocolate mixture, then pour into the pastry case.

Bake in the preheated oven at 200°C (400°F, Gas mark 6), for about 40–50 minutes until puffed, set around the edges, but still wobbly in the centre. Serve warm or cold dusted with icing sugar and with ice cream or cream.

Orange-flower Cheese Tart

Orange-flower water was substituted for rose water in some English dishes towards the end of the 17th century. Few English gardens had fallen orange blossoms to make this scented water, so it was usually imported from France or Portugal. Both orange-flower and rose water continued in popularity as food flavourings all through the 18th century, but then lost favour. Recently, there has been a renewed interest and they can be bought at grocers or chemists. Bake this tart the day before serving.

serves 12

225g (8oz) digestive biscuits
225g (8oz) butter
700g (1lb 9oz) cream cheese
225g (8oz) caster sugar
3 eggs

1 teaspoon orange-flower water
1 level tablespoon orange zest
150ml (¼ pint) soured cream
fresh orange segments,
  for decorating

Put the biscuits in a plastic bag and crush with a rolling pin. Melt 115g (4oz) butter and mix together with the biscuit crumbs in a mixing bowl. Press into a 23cm (9in) spring-release cake tin to cover the base. Place in the refrigerator while making filling.

In a large mixing bowl, beat the cream cheese until smooth. Slowly beat in the sugar until evenly blended. Add the remaining butter, melted in a small saucepan, beaten eggs, orange-flower water and orange zest. Continue beating until the mixture is really smooth. Pour into the chilled crumb base. Bake in the centre of a preheated oven at 150°C (300°F, Gas mark 2) for 45 minutes. Turn off the oven, but leave the cheesecake in the oven for a further 30 minutes. Remove from the oven and cool. Leave in a cool place overnight if possible.

To serve, remove the sides of the tin and loosen the cheesecake from the base with a palette knife. Slide it on to a plate and spread the top with soured cream. Decorate with fresh orange segments.

Manchester Tart

Also called Manchester Pudding, as its original form in the 18th century would have been made in a deep pie dish lined around the side with pastry.

serves
6

175g (6oz) shortcrust pastry

for the filling
300ml (½ pint) full-cream milk
zest of 1 lemon
50g (1¾oz) fresh white breadcrumbs
2 large eggs, separated
50g (1¾oz) butter, melted
1 tablespoon brandy
100g (3¾oz) caster sugar
3 tablespoons good-quality jam
    of your choice

Roll out the pastry and use to line a buttered 20cm (8in) pie plate or shallow flan tin. Bake blind in the usual way.

To make the filling, bring the milk to the boil in a pan with the lemon zest. Remove from the heat and allow to cool so that the flavour of the lemon will infuse with the milk. Pour the cooled milk through a sieve over the breadcrumbs. Beat the egg yolks into the mixture, then add the melted butter, brandy and 25g (1oz) of the sugar. Spread your chosen jam on to the bottom of the pastry case and pour over the filling.

Bake in a preheated oven at 180°C (350°F, Gas mark 4) for 40–45 minutes. While the tart is cooking, whisk the egg whites with half the remaining sugar until stiff, then fold in the rest of the sugar. Coat the top of the tart with this meringue, then put back in the oven for about 15 minutes until crisp and lightly browned.

Treacle Tart

With the setting up of sugar refineries in British ports in the late 18th century, treacle, the syrup remaining after the sugar had been refined, became generally available. The origin of treacle tart may be medieval gingerbread, which was made by pressing breadcrumbs, treacle, spices and colourings together. Treacle was later replaced in tarts by golden syrup, but the name remained. In the north it continued to be popular as it was a cheaper sweetener.

serves
6

175g (6oz) shortcrust, sweet shortcrust or almond pastry

for the filling
50g (1¾oz) fresh white breadcrumbs
zest and juice of 1 lemon
½ teaspoon ground ginger
6 tablespoons golden syrup
3 tablespoons double cream

Chill the pastry, then roll out thinly and use to line a buttered 20cm (8in) shallow loose-bottomed flan tin. Prick all over and chill for at about 30 minutes, then bake blind. Remove from the oven and cool briefly.

Mix the filling ingredients together and pour into the pastry case. Bake in a preheated oven at 200°C (400°F, Gas mark 6) for 5 minutes, then reduce to 160°C (325°F, Gas mark 3). Bake for a further 25 minutes, or until golden brown and set.

Remove from the oven and leave to cool for at least 30 minutes, then serve warm with custard, ice cream or cream.

Lady's Tart

This 19th-century tart was originally filled with apricot preserve and decorated with flaked almonds. It had a decorative edge of small pastry circles. In this recipe, I have used four varieties of jam laid in sections and divided by strips of pastry – once the pride of housewives, who, of course, used their best homemade jams.

serves
6

225g (8oz) shortcrust pastry
2 tablespoons apricot jam
2 tablespoons raspberry or
    strawberry jam
2 tablespoons blackcurrant jam
2 tablespoons green gooseberry
    or greengage jam
milk or water, for brushing
1 egg, beaten
1 tablespoon cold water

Roll out the pastry thinly and use two-thirds of it to line a buttered 25cm (10in) ovenproof plate. Divide the pastry base into 8 sections, marking lightly with a knife. Spread each section with the different jams alternating the colours and avoiding the rim of the plate. Cut the pastry trimmings into narrow strips and arrange in twists across the tart dividing the jams.

Cut the remaining one-third of the pastry into small circles with a 2.5cm (1in) cutter. Brush the rim of the pastry-lined plate with a little milk or water and arrange the circles around the edge, overlapping them a little.

Beat the egg with the water and brush the pastry circles and twists carefully to glaze. Bake in the centre of a preheated oven at 190°C (375°F, Gas mark 5) for about 30 minutes or until pastry is golden brown. Serve hot or cold with custard, or thick cream.

Index

Numerals in *italics* refer to photographs